# The Most
# WONDERFUL
# DOLLHOUSE BOOK

# The Most WONDERFUL DOLLHOUSE BOOK

Easy-To-Make, Inexpensive Houses
with Furnishings
and Lovable Doll Families

## MILLIE HINES

c/wB.

Butterick Publishing

# Acknowledgments

Special thanks to my sister Janet Hines. Thanks also to Frank Hendricks, Jack Tynan, Bill Newman, and Frances Curran for typing and testing instructions. And thanks to my cousins Rachel, 7, and Michael, 4, and to my nieces Cathy, 2, Patty, 1, and Kristin, 1 month, for inspiration. My appreciation to Evelyn Brannon and to my editor Carol Castellano.

CREDITS

| Illustrations | Photography | Book Design |
|---|---|---|
| Millie Hines | Edward Scibetta | Sallie Baldwin |

Library of Congress Cataloging in Publication Data

Hines, Millie.
    The most wonderful dollhouse book.
    Includes index.
    1. Doll-houses.    2. Dollmaking.    I. Title.
TT175.3.H56      745.59′23      78-11766
      ISBN 0-88421-076-6

Copyright © 1979 by Butterick Publishing
708 Third Avenue
New York, New York 10017
A Division of American Can Company

Manufactured and printed in the United States of America.
Published simultaneously in the USA and Canada.

# Contents

# Welcome to the Wonderful Dollhouse

A dollhouse is a special part of childhood. Children have been known to sit entranced for hours and hours arranging and rearranging the furniture, preparing meals of pretend food, and inventing ingenious ways for their dolls to spend the day. The dollhouses in this book are designed to stimulate a child's creativity and imagination. There are simple houses for younger children and more involved ones designed to keep older children interested and happy.

The basic house is made very simply from a cardboard box. It can be folded flat for storage. One house/box can be used alone—as a cottage, studio apartment, or a schoolhouse, for example—or two or three boxes can be stacked and reinforced for sturdiness to make a two-story house or a three-story town house. Would you be able to guess that all of the dollhouses pictured in the book are made from the same simple design? They look so different only because the walls and floors and furnishings are different. As you can see, when you make your own dollhouse the possibilities are endless and beautiful results are easy to achieve.

The equipment you'll need is simple, too—an X-Acto knife, a straightedge, and a few household items like a pair of scissors, glue, and tape. A complete list of materials appears at the beginning of each project.

The houses are designed so that the furnishings can be arranged in many different ways. The Color Plates, beginning on page 97, will give you some ideas to start you off and you and your child are sure to have fun thinking up ideas of your own. An introduction to floor plans and interior design for children is included as well.

The scale of the houses and dolls is approximately 1½″ = 1′. This scale makes everything 50 percent larger than in standard dollhouses and in official child-testing done in my living room, the large scale also makes the houses a perfect size for children to play with! Since many everyday items such as milk containers, thread spools, and paper cups fit comfortably into this scale, the making of furniture and accessories is much easier than in the true miniature size.

The houses and dolls are intended to be made by adults or older children, but there are many projects included for young children to work on. These projects are specially marked in the book as "Learn-Tos." When I was a little girl I would especially have liked the idea of changeable sheets, slipcovers, and quilts. In fact, my mother recently showed me a doll's bedcover I made when I was five years old. I had crayoned flowers onto a handkerchief. Your child might like to to try this, too, or perhaps you would like to color the Star of Bethlehem quilt on page 52.

To make a house a home, a dollhouse needs a family. I have designed special cloth dolls that are lovable, dressable, and safe even for little children to play with. There are two types to choose from, and you can decide which type to make according to the age of your child and how much time you want to spend making them. Patterns for the dolls and their clothing are full size and easy to use.

Sweet little baby dolls with layettes and furniture may fit into your dolls' plans. Maybe your dolls would also enjoy the company of a dog or a cat. Patterns for these are included, too, and also patterns for a delightful family of bears to make from felt.

This book is full of ideas and patterns for doll clothing, pretend food, dishes, pots and pans, kitchen appliances, furniture for every room, and more. With them you can construct dollhouses and furnishings that are prettier and more fun to play with than any that money can buy. You can spend just a few hours or develop a lifelong hobby. And hopefully you can make a dream come true for a little child in *your* house.

# part one
# DOLLHOUSES

# Making
# the Basic House

A few simple cuts can transform a 16″ X 16″ X 20″ cardboard moving carton into a foldable dollhouse that's the perfect size for children to play with. Most moving companies will sell such cartons to you even if you aren't moving. (Mine were from Allied and cost $1.50 each.) You can also pick up free cartons at stores, but they may be of a size that is not as easy to work with. The building instructions in the book refer to 16″ X 16″ X 20″ moving boxes. You can adapt the instructions for different size boxes.

Your dollhouse can be as simple or as complex as you like. Start off with a basic one-story house (see

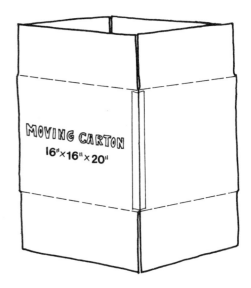

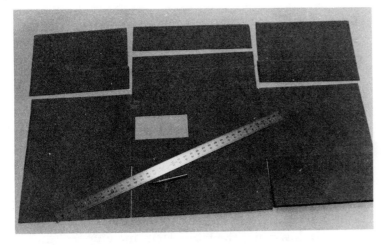

**A few simple cuts transform a box into a dollhouse.**

Color Plate 3) or indulge your taste for the sophisticated with a grand, two- or three-story house (see Color Plates 13 and 14). You will need one moving box for each floor.

MATERIALS

Cardboard moving box (or boxes) 16″ X 16″ X 20″ (These boxes come flat.)

Two 3″ X 3″ scraps of a medium-weight fabric for side flap hinges

White glue

Two large brass paper fasteners or two ⁶⁄₃₂″ X ¾″ stove bolts and nuts

EQUIPMENT

Sharp pencil

X-Acto knife with no. 11 blade

Tape measure or ruler

Metal yardstick or wide straightedge of metal, plywood, or fiberboard

## CONSTRUCTING THE DOLLHOUSE

Each floor of the house is made from one moving box. For every story you want to construct, follow the instructions below *once*. When you build a three-story house, however, first read the section on page 30, since the depth of this house is different from the one- and two-story versions.

SPECIAL HINTS FOR CONSTRUCTION

- Before you cut cardboard, put down a layer of cardboard or a heavy layer of newspapers in an even thickness to protect your table or floor.
- If you use a wide straightedge it will keep your fingers well out of the path of the X-Acto knife.
- When you cut cardboard with an X-Acto knife, it isn't necessary to press hard enough to cut through on the first pass. Two or three easy cuts along the same line work just as well and are easier to make.
- If you are using a larger cardboard box and need to cut it down, use the fabric strip and glue technique, page 20, to rejoin the sections. It works better than tape.

- Keep all of the leftover cardboard pieces. They can be used later for spare floors, a roof, room dividers, kitchen splashboards, etc.

1. Cut the box open along the paper-taped side (figure 1-1). Open it out flat.

2. Using the straightedge as a guide, cut off one 20″ side (figure 1-2).

3. The inside of the box becomes the inside of the house. Measure 4″ down from the flap fold on the two side pieces. (The 4″ left on the center piece eventually forms the alcove overhang in the back section of the house.) Mark and cut. On the 16″ box this leaves a 12″ high wall (this measurement can vary slightly) (figure 1-3).

4. Measure 3″ up from flap fold on the center piece and cut across (figure 1-3).

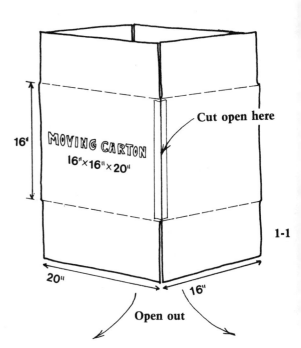

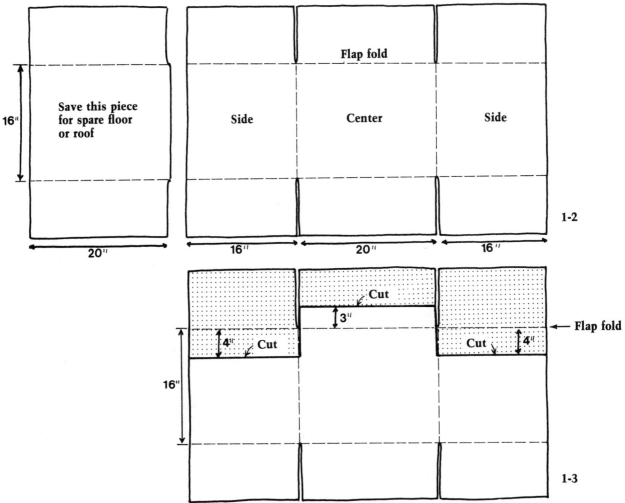

5. Form the alcove overhang by folding the center extension down. To make the fold line, score the cardboard so it can be bent (figure 1-4). One light cut should do, since you don't want to cut all the way through.

- Before making the score line, practice first on a scrap of cardboard.

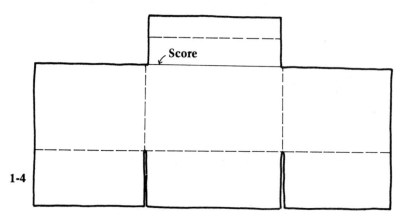

1-4

6. Cut two 3" X 3¾" cardboard pieces for the overhang side tabs out of the small strip left over from the top of the center section (figure 1–5).

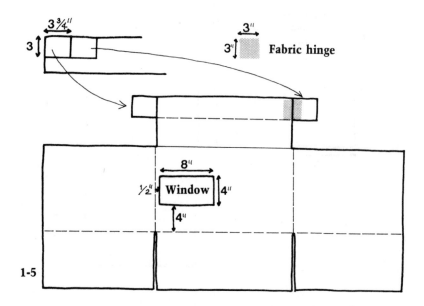

1-5

7. Hinge the side tabs to the alcove overhang by gluing the 3" squares of fabric to the cardboard (figure 1-5). Let the glue dry thoroughly.

8. Cut out a 4" X 8" window at the location shown (figure 1-5).

9. If you are building a three-story house, turn to page 30 and follow the instructions for cutting down the depth of the walls. You must do this before covering the walls.

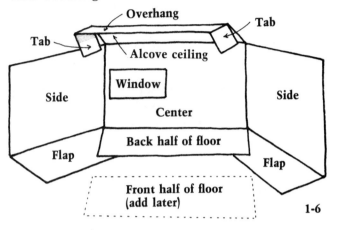

1-6

## COVERING THE WALLS

The wall coverings you use will set the mood of your dollhouse. The Color Plates illustrate a wide variety of looks, from the casual simplicity of the Bears' house (Color Plate 21) to the elegant and elaborate decor of the Prince and Princess's castle (Color Plate 17).

Before you begin, consider the many possibilities. You can construct a one-, two-, or three-story house with as many rooms as you like. You can use the same wall covering for several rooms or a different one in each. You can choose fabric, paper, or self-adhesive plastic (Con-Tact paper) or combine them in a house. Here are some elements to consider:

- Printed fabrics and calicos make colorful walls. You can coordinate your dollhouse interior by using the same print fabric for closets, slipcovers, pillows, and accessories.

- Solid colored fabric and paper tend to show imperfections in cardboard and gluing, so prints will look neater. It's better to use self-adhesive plastic when you want solid colors.

- One package of gift wrap (two 20" X 28" sheets) is just the right amount for one dollhouse. If you can find nice patterns on gift wrap rolls you can avoid the creases of the folded paper. Many of the especially nice imported gift wraps come only in sheets. The sophisticated two-story house (Color Plate 13) is decorated with imported museum reproduction gift wrap, but it cost only 60¢ a package.

- Con-Tact paper comes in solid colors, prints, and wood grains.
- White walls provide a neutral background for many changeable room styles.

**Note:** If you decide to make a three-story house, you must cut down the depth of the walls of each box *before you cover them* with a wall covering. Follow the instructions for Two- and Three-Story Houses, page 30.

Whether you use fabric, paper, or Con-Tact paper, the application steps are basically the same. But before you begin, note the following hints about each one.

### Fabric or Paper Application

Apply fabric and paper with white glue or a fusible web.

- Since fabric is absorbent, you will need more glue for fabric than for paper. It's a good idea to do a sample first to get the feel of it.
- To use glue, apply it at the edge of the wall (not over the whole surface), then smooth it with your finger into a strip about ½" wide. Position the fabric or paper over the cardboard and smooth it down.
- Sometimes the cardboard curves up as it dries. If this happens, just iron the bare cardboard side on a steam-wool setting until it is straight again.
- Using fusible web takes longer than gluing but the results are smoother and more even. Be sure to do a sample before you work on your actual house. You'll need about 2½ yards of web. Cut the pieces of web the same size as the fabric or paper pieces. Fuse one surface at a time, layering cardboard, web, fabric or paper. Iron on a steam-wool setting until fused.
- When you fuse paper to cardboard, put a piece of scrap fabric over the paper when ironing to prevent the printed design from smearing.

## Con-Tact Paper Application

● An extra pair of hands is helpful for applying Con-Tact paper. Have a friend hold up one end of the piece while you place yours down near the fold line, then gradually smooth down the piece from the fold line out.

STEP-BY-STEP: Any Wall Covering

1. Cut the wall covering you have chosen according to the layouts.

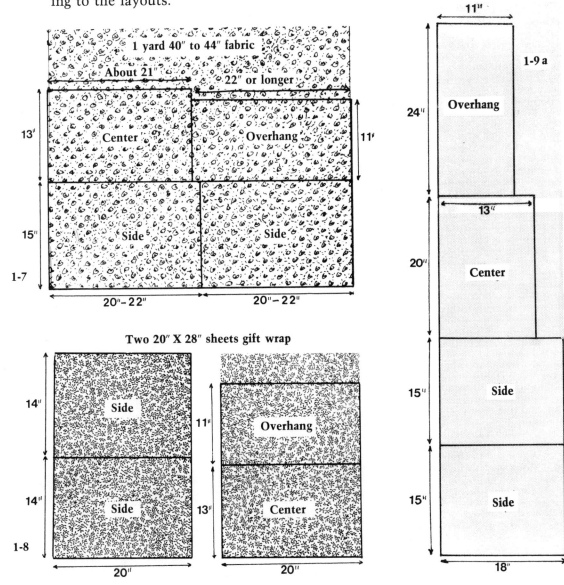

Solid color Con-Tact paper

11"

1-9 a

24"

Overhang

13"

20"

Center

15"

Side

15"

Side

18"

1 yard 40" to 44" fabric

About 21"

22" or longer

13"

Center

Overhang

11"

15"

Side

Side

1-7

20"-22"

20"-22"

Two 20" X 28" sheets gift wrap

14"

Side

11"

Overhang

14"

Side

13"

Center

1-8

20"

20"

Directional print Con-Tact paper

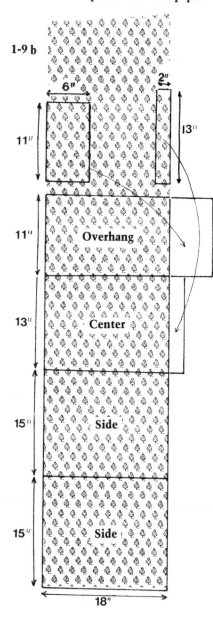

1-9 b

6"  2"

11"  13"

11"  **Overhang**

13"  **Center**

15"  **Side**

15"  **Side**

18"

2. Bring the wall covering to within ⅛" of the side fold (figure 1-10). (Bringing it to the center of the fold will cause wrinkles.) For a perfectly straight fabric edge, use either a selvage, cut edge, or single fold—whatever works best for your fabric. The wall covering extends about 1" below the floor line.

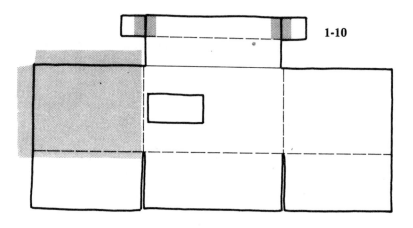

1-10

3. Gradually smooth down the piece from the side fold line out.

4. Cut away the corner (figure 1-10). Turn the box so that the outside faces you. First fold over the top, then the side edges of the wall covering (figure 1-11).

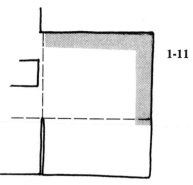

1-11

5. After covering both sides, cover the center section. The center piece should reach to within ⅛" of the side folds to allow for bending (figure 1-12).

- Cut fabric to fit or fold the side edges under to fit.
- Gift wrap will either be just the right width or will need a little trimming.

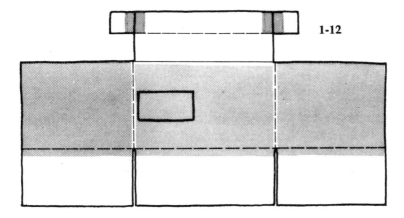

1-12

- Directional Con-Tact paper prints have to be pieced. All other center section coverings are in one piece.
- Cut Con-Tact paper to fit *before* removing the backing.

6. Apply the top overhang covering piece by pressing or gluing it in place. Clip (figure 1-13).

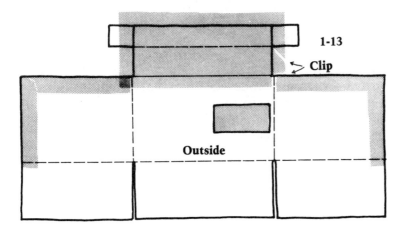

1-13

Clip

Outside

7. Fold the covering around the tab and attach it (figure 1-14).

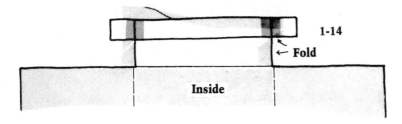

1-14

← Fold

Inside

8. Make an opening in the covering for the window by slitting to the window corners from the outside. Glue fabric or press Con-Tact paper in place on the outside of the house (figure 1-15).

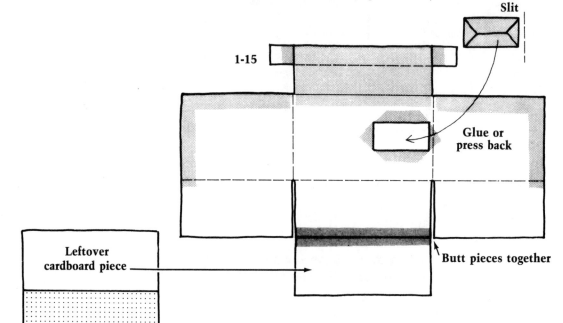

**1-15**

Slit

Glue or press back

Leftover cardboard piece

Butt pieces together

## THE FLOOR

The next step in the dollhouse construction is to complete the floor. Since the flap that is at the bottom does not cover the full floor area, you'll have to add another piece of cardboard to get a full-size floor.

There are several possibilities of floor coverings—permanent ones like fabric, paper, and Con-Tact paper, and changeable ones like scarf or hand towel rugs.

### Floor Construction
STEP-BY-STEP

1. Have the house flat, outside facing you.

2. To extend the floor to the full 20″ X 16″ size, cut a flap along the fold line from a leftover cardboard piece.

3. Butt the floor pieces together (figure 1-15).

- If you are going to cover the floor with fabric or paper, join the butted sections with a 3″ wide fabric strip that runs the width of the floor. Put a generous amount of glue on the cardboard, then lay on the fabric strip and smooth it down. Allow it to dry thoroughly.

- If you are going to install a Con-Tact paper floor, you can use a 3″ Con-Tact paper strip instead of fabric as tape to hold the floor sections together.

4. Set up the house to mark the floor edge. Flatten the box again and trim the floor along the marked edge (figure 1-16).

## Permanent Floor Coverings

STEP-BY-STEP

1. Cut an 18″ X 24″ rectangle of material (figure 1-17).

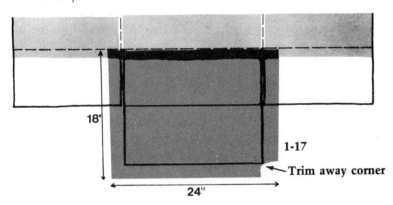

18″

1-17

Trim away corner

24″

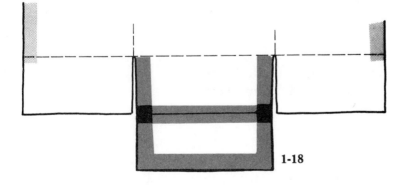

1-16

2. Position the covering within ⅛″ of the back fold, to allow for bending (figure 1-17).

- Follow the instructions and hints for wall coverings, page 15, to attach your material to the cardboard.

3. Fold the floor covering around to the outside and attach it (figure 1-18).

1-18

4. Apply a floor protector to fabric or paper floors (optional). Please be careful with this substance if your child is helping with the project.

- A clear acrylic finish gives a linoleum look. This finish can darken fabric and paper, however, so do a sample first.
- You can spray fabric floors with a fabric protector.
- A clear piece of Con-Tact paper will protect a paper floor.

## Changeable Floor Coverings

*Rug Remnant (Color Plate 13)*

Cut the carpet to the same size as the floor, 16" X 20", by marking the size on the back of the carpet, then cutting with an X-Acto knife and a straightedge. Most carpets are firm enough to be set in the box without any attachment.

*Fake Fur or Fluffy Rug Remnant*

Cut the piece to the 16" X 20" size. If the piece is too light to hold the shape, glue it to the spare floor (see next page).

*Hand Towel (Color Plate 2)*

Hand towels are usually just the right size (about 16" X 24") simply to be tucked under the floor at each end.

*Scarf*

A paisley head scarf makes a beautiful Oriental rug. Attach it as for other fabric (see page 16) to the original or spare floor (page 23) or just tuck the edges under.

*Fabric Throw Rugs (Color Plate 21)*

To make a throw or area rug, simply cut squares or rectangles of fabric. Unravel the edges to make fringe. Miniature scarf print fabrics make particularly nice rugs—see the living room of the town house (Color Plate 14).

*Pot Holder Throw Rugs (Color Plate 8)*

You can sew two or more pot holders together to

make colorful throw rugs. Children enjoy weaving the pot holders. Looms and loops for them are available at five-and-tens.

## Spare Floor

A spare floor comes in handy when your child has the urge to redecorate the dollhouse. You can cover the spare floor in any material—even cover both sides of it in different materials—and have a quick and easy way to change the look of a room.

**An unfurnished house with a spare floor.**

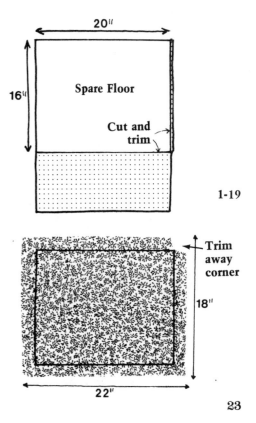

1-19

STEP-BY-STEP

1. Cut the flap from the spare floor carton piece. The cut-down piece should measure 16″ X 20″ (figure 1-19).

2. Cover this spare floor using an 18″ X 22″ or larger piece of material and one of the floor covering methods on page 21 (figure 1-19).

• You can also make a reversible slipcover for the spare floor in two different fabrics. Trace the outline of the floor onto the wrong side of the fabric. Sew around the pencil line on three sides and turn right sides out. Insert the floor, tuck the fabric edges in, and sew the slipcover opening closed.

23

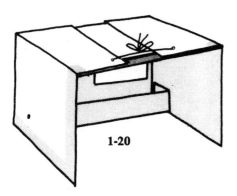

**1-20**

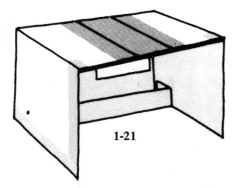

**1-21**

## SECURING THE BOTTOM OF THE BOX
## (Figure 1-20)

STEP-BY-STEP

1. Turn the house upside down. Punch holes in the bottom flaps, about 2″ from the corners.

2. Tie the flaps together under the box with a string through the holes. This string and the fasteners or bolts at the sides of the overhang hold the house together. When it's time to fold the house for storage, simply remove them.

If you do not intend to fold the house away very often, you can cut a piece of cardboard to fit between the flaps and fasten the sections together with wide tape or a wide strip of Con-Tact paper instead of using the string (figure 1-21). It is wise to finish the bottom of a two- or three-story house in this way to give it extra strength.

## FOLDING THE HOUSE FOR STORAGE

To fold the house first fold the sides toward the center, then the floor toward the back (figure 1-22).

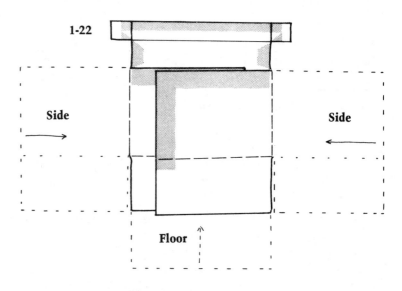

**1-22**

Side

Side

Floor

## ROOM DIVIDER

The room divider is a very useful item in the dollhouse. Since it fits anywhere under the alcove overhang, it can be moved to one side or another to remodel the house's interior. It can separate the kitchen from the living room or bedroom in a one-floor house (see Color Plate 4) or it can be the wall between two bedrooms in a two-story model (Color Plate 10). You could place it very near the outside wall to make a little storage space, too.

STEP-BY-STEP

1. Cut the room divider from a leftover cardboard flap, cutting a ¼" slot 2½" long in the center top (figure 1-23).

2. Cover both sides of the room divider with wall or floor covering material. Use a 12½" X 16" piece of covering. Trim away the corners, fold back, and attach the covering (figure 1-23).

3. Cut the slot through the covering material.

4. Slip the room divider along the front of the alcove overhang (figure 1-24).

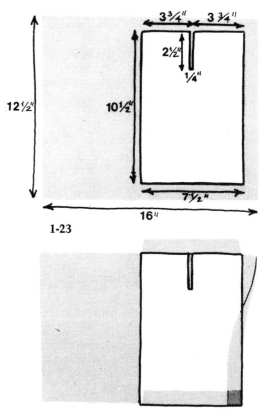

1-23

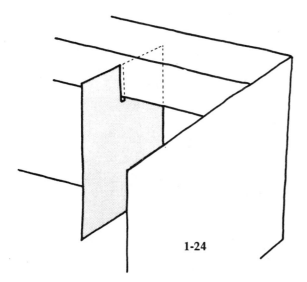

1-24

## WINDOW TREATMENTS

The windows in the dollhouse can provide atmosphere and become a delightful play area for children. You may be able to duplicate the windows of your real home or put in a style you have always admired. The house and doll family can be transported to the far corners of the world—or even to other galaxies—through the addition of scenic and other imaginative picture views. The child who'd love a window seat can place a comfortable sofa beneath a clear "glass" window and settle the dolls there to relax and read a book or gaze dreamily out at the view.

## Picture Window (Color Plate 21)

Tape a piece of clear plastic vinyl (it comes on rolls at the five-and-ten) or a piece of acetate (from a box with a plastic cover) to the back of the house to cover the window area. The result is a bright picture window that lets the sun shine in.

**Diamond-shaped Window Lattice Pattern, next page**

## Diamond-shaped Window Lattice (Color Plate 10)

Ten thin wooden coffee stirrers or popsicle sticks make a lovely lattice for the window.

STEP-BY-STEP
1. Trace or photocopy the lattice pattern.
2. Place a piece of waxed paper over the pattern sheet. Arrange and glue the stirrers or the sticks on the waxed paper. After the glue is thoroughly dry, remove the lattice from the paper.
3. Tape or glue the lattice to the outside of the house behind the window opening. Then place a piece of clear plastic behind the lattice.

## Lace Curtain (Color Plate 14)

Give your house an old-fashioned or traditional feeling with a lace curtain. Cut out a piece of crocheted lace or use a doily to cover the window area. Tape or glue the lace or doily behind the window opening.

## Window with a View (Color Plate 23)

A printed picture taped behind the window opening becomes an instant scenic view.

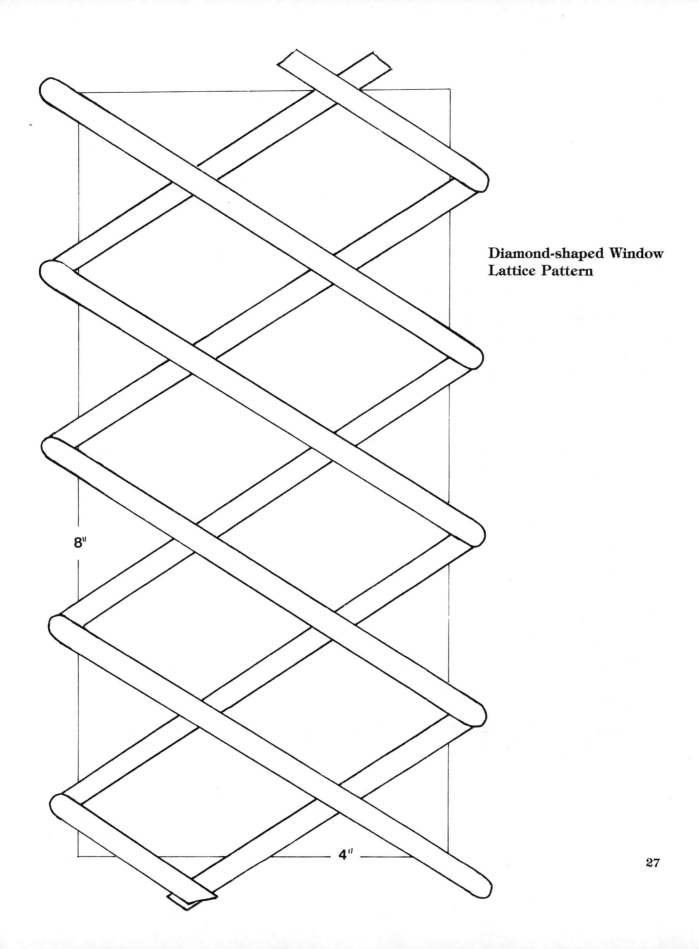

Diamond-shaped Window
Lattice Pattern

8"

4"

## SETTING UP A ONE-STORY HOUSE FOR PLAY

The dollhouse can be set up in several ways—with closed sides (see Color Plate 4), with either wing partially open (see Color Plate 5), or with either wing fully open (see Color Plate 7). Your child can play with the house closed one day and opened out the next—remodeling is simple!

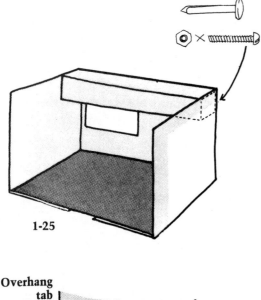

**1-25**

STEP-BY-STEP: House with Closed Sides

1. Fold in the alcove overhang.

2. Attach the side walls to the tabs with paper fasteners or nuts and bolts (figure 1-25). To mark where to put the fasteners or bolts, hold the overhang in place and stick a straight pin through both overhang and wall. Make a small slit with an X-Acto knife for a paper fastener or make a small X for bolts. Then insert the fasteners or bolts and secure.

STEP-BY-STEP: House with a Wing

1. Cut a 2″ X 3″ rectangle from a leftover piece of cardboard. Butt it against the overhang tab on the side that you choose to have open (figure 1-26 a).

2. Cover the piece and the tab with wall covering.

3. Attach the new elongated tab to the outside back of the house with a paper fastener or bolt (figure 1-26 c).

4. Cover the floor flap with material (see page 21) (figure 1-26 c).

Figure 1-27 shows a house with the wing completely open.

**Overhang tab**

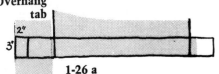

2″

3′

**1-26 a**

**Elongated tab**

**1-26 b**

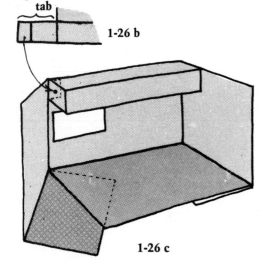

**1-26 c**

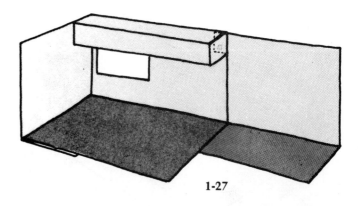

**1-27**

## TWO- AND THREE-STORY HOUSES

Two- or three-story houses can be lots of fun, especially for older children, since they allow even more opportunity for furniture and room rearrangement. (See An Introduction to Floor Plans, page 89.) With the addition of a simple Room Divider, page 24, the dollhouse can become a two- or three-bedroom model. You can decorate each bedroom with different wall and floor coverings and add new furniture to achieve many eye-pleasing looks. The best part is that the two- and three-story houses are truly easy to make.

Multi-story houses are simply two or three boxes stacked up. Construction is the same except for a decrease in the depth of the three-story town house. Wood molding strips reinforce and connect the boxes to make them very sturdy.

### REINFORCEMENT MATERIALS

Use ⅝" or ¾" quarter-round molding (figure 1-28) or ¾" square baluster (figure 1-29) reinforcements for multi-story houses. You can get these inexpensively at any lumber yard. Buy the wood a little longer than you need. Then measure and saw the wood to exactly the same width as the floor of the house (figure 1-30). They are easy to cut with a small hand saw.

You will need one strip for the two-story house and three strips for the three-story (two for floor reinforcements, one for the roof). You will also need ½" wire nails.

STEP-BY-STEP: Attaching the Wooden Reinforcements
1. To attach the wood strip, have the alcove overhang assembled. Move the floor up out of the way and position the wood under the flaps making sure the floor will fit back down again (figure 1-31).
2. Attach the wood with ½" wire nails.
3. To connect the stories, nail or screw through the box into each end of the wood strip, placing the nails or screws carefully so they are centered in the wood on each end (figure 1-32). If you are using screws you may want to make small guide holes in the wood.
- For the two-story, place the upper box opening 6" from the front (figure 1-32). This recessed

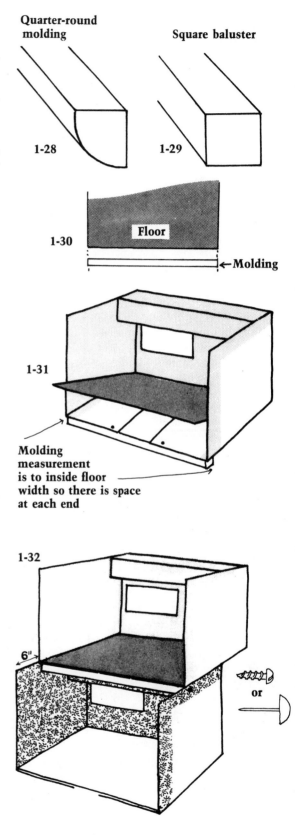

Quarter-round molding

Square baluster

1-28

1-29

1-30

Floor

←Molding

1-31

Molding measurement is to inside floor width so there is space at each end

1-32

6"

or

stacking provides an open and comfortable play area. (When the 16″ deep boxes are stacked directly on top of each other it is hard to reach into the bottom box.)

- For the three-story, the boxes must be stacked directly on top of one another. Since this makes the play area difficult to reach, it is better to cut the depth of each story from 16″ to 13″ (figure 1-33). Cut the walls down before applying the

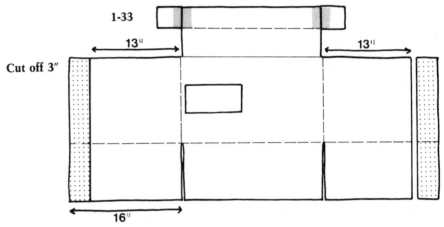

1-33

Cut off 3″  13″  13″  16″

wall covering. Attach the wood to the bottoms of the second and third stories (figure 1-34). Stack the boxes directly on top of each other and nail or screw the box sides to the wood, one story at a time.

## SECURING THE BOTTOM OF THE BOX

Refer to the instructions for securing the bottom of the single-story house, page 24. It is a good idea to add the extra strip of cardboard to the underside of two- and three-story houses to give them extra strength.

## A ROOF FOR THE DOLLHOUSE
### (Color Plates 13 and 14)

You can give your dollhouse a crowning glory by topping it off with an elegant shingled roof. Easily made out of cardboard, the roof is permanent on the town house and removable on one- or two-story houses (because it is easier to play in the open-topped house

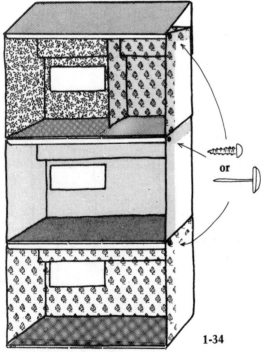

or

1-34

than to reach in under the roof). The town house roof measures 20″ across; the removable roof measures 23″ across.

For each of the boxes you used you will have a large leftover piece which is labeled "save this piece for spare floor or roof" (see page 13). Use one of these for the roof, leaving one flap attached at the back.

MATERIALS FOR THE TOWN HOUSE ROOF
> Corrugated cardboard roof piece 20″ X 21″
> Lightweight grey cardboard, oaktag, or manila for shingles
> One wooden reinforcement strip (see page 29)
> White glue
> Paper fasteners or nuts and bolts
> Nails or screws

MATERIALS FOR THE REMOVABLE ROOF
> Corrugated cardboard roof piece 23″ X 21″
> Lightweight grey cardboard, oaktag, or manila for shingles
> White glue
> String

STEP-BY-STEP: Constructing the Roof
> 1. Make a template for the shingles by tracing the pattern below first onto tracing paper and then onto lightweight cardboard.

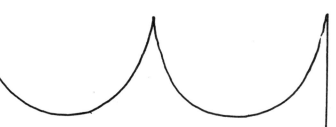

**Shingle Pattern
for Three-Story House**

**Shingle Pattern for
One- or Two-Story House**

**Trace and cut**

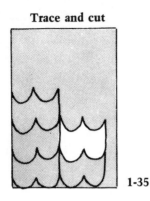

1-35

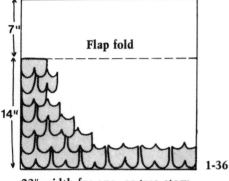

1-36

23″ width for one- or two-story house

20″ width for three-story

2. Trace and cut out 42 shingles from grey cardboard, oaktag, or manila (figure 1-35).

- Using slightly different shades of grey cardboard gives a natural slate look.

3. Starting at the lower edge and placing the last row at the fold line, arrange seven rows of shingles on the roof piece *before gluing* to get an idea of the spacing that looks best (figure 1-36). Use half shingles at the end of every other row. Mark the rows in pencil on the roof, then remove the shingles.

STEP-BY-STEP: Attaching the Town House Roof

1. Cut the wooden reinforcement piece to the same width as the floor (see page 29). Center it under the bottom edge of the roof and nail or screw it in place (figure 1-37).

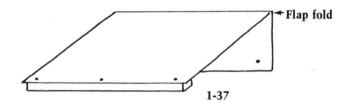

Flap fold

1-37

2. Cut a 2″ X 20″ strip of your shingle material and glue it along the bottom of the roof (figure 1-36).

3. Glue the shingles on with white glue, starting with the bottom row (figure 1-36).

4. The flap fold is the peak of the roof. Attach the back roof flap to the back of the house with paper fasteners or nuts and bolts.

5. Nail or screw the top corner of the house to the wood.

STEP-BY-STEP: Attaching the Removable Roof

1. Cut a 2″ X 23″ strip of your shingle material and glue it along the bottom of the roof (figure 1-36).

2. Glue the shingles on with white glue starting from the bottom row (figure 1-36).

3. Punch holes in the roof and in the back flap. Thread a piece of string through the holes on both sides to hold the roof at an angle (figure 1-38).

4. Place the roof on the house.

**Flap fold**

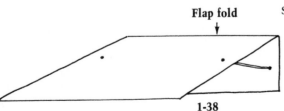

1-38

# WOOD-REINFORCED DOLLHOUSE

If you would like the look and added durability of a wooden dollhouse you can reinforce the cardboard sides and floors with fiberboard or ¼″ plywood (figure 1-39).

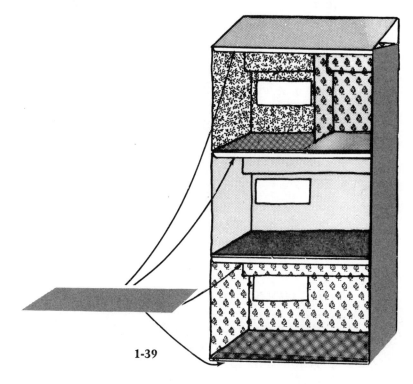

1-39

MATERIALS

Two 2′ X 4′ pieces of ¼″ plywood or fiberboard
Paint or Con-Tact paper to cover
White glue

STEP-BY-STEP

1. Cut out the pieces you need according to figure 1-40.
- The floor and roof pieces measure 11″ by the width of the floor.
2. Cover or paint the side pieces.
3. Glue the wood reinforcement pieces on with white glue.

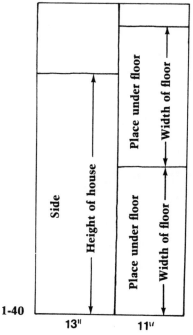

1-40

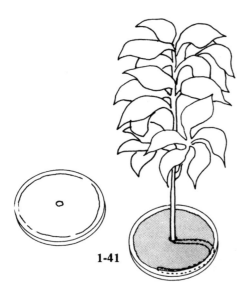

**1-41**

## YARD (Color Plate 5)

An expanse of lawn beautifully landscaped with flowers and trees and shrubbery for a dollhouse? It's easy to do and lots of fun to play with. The dolls can have picnics in the yard and the pets can have plenty of space to run and play.

Reversible green indoor-outdoor carpet provides both a wonderful large yard and a comfortable place for children to sit while at play. A yard or two of 3' wide runner is enough. Plastic turf is fine for small yards (Color Plate 17) but its surface is too rough for sitting.

To make movable trees, bend the bottom of the stem of a 12" plastic plant sprig. Poke a hole through a plastic lid and insert the stem through the hole (figure 1-41). Glue the stem to the lid. For more permanent trees, insert the bent stem under the carpet lawn.

To make flagstones, cut the shapes out of grey cardboard and arrange them as a walkway.

## DOGHOUSE (Color Plate 14)

What you need in your lovely yard is a doghouse. Children love this addition and the pets who live in it. (On pages 196 and 198 you can learn to make dogs and cats.) When you're through building you might want to place the name of your pet over the doorway.

MATERIALS
    Half-gallon milk container
    Ball point pen
    6" X 18" piece of Con-Tact paper for walls
    6" X 6" piece of Con-Tact paper for roof
    Acrylic paint (optional, for name)

STEP-BY-STEP
    1. Measure and mark the dimensions on the milk container. Press hard with a ball point pen to make the fold lines (figure 1-42).
    2. Cut and fold (figure 1-43).
    3. Lean the roof sections in and mark the peak on each piece. Press along the line with a pen to make the fold line. Fold each piece over at the peak. Tape.

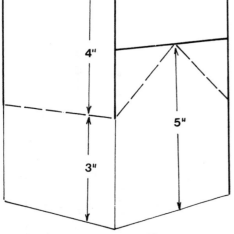

**1-42**

4. Cover the sides with Con-Tact paper. Clip and fit it in place (figure 1-44).

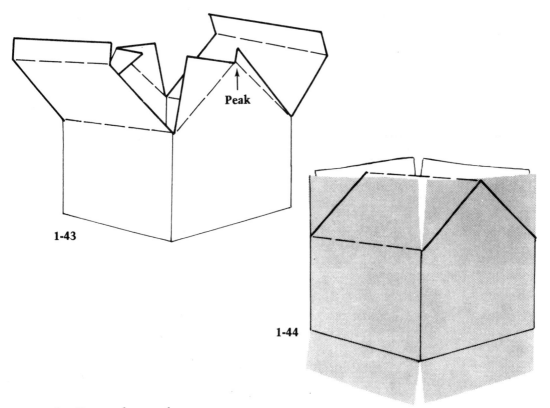

**1-43**

**Peak**

**1-44**

5. Cover the roof.

6. Draw the outline of the doorway on the Con-Tact paper. Cut the opening out with manicure scissors.

7. If you'd like to, paint the dog's name over the doorway (figure 1-45).

**1-45**

# 2
# Furnishing
# the Living Room

The idea behind *The Most Wonderful Dollhouse Book* is to show you how to make easy, large-scale dollhouses that are fun for children of any age to play with. Therefore there's a lot of flexibility designed into the houses themselves and the furnishings for them. If you look through the Color Plates you will see that it's possible to furnish a dollhouse with as few as six elements (see the simple Bear house, Color Plate 21). It's also possible to divide the same one-box house into

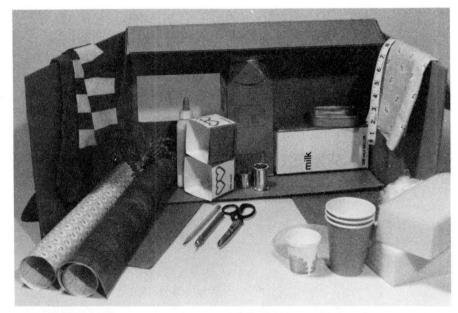

**The furnishings are easy to make out of household materials.**

two (Color Plate 22) or even three rooms (Color Plate 7). You can make dollhousekeeping as simple or as involved as you like.

Since the living room in the simpler houses becomes the bedroom at night, and since these houses can have the dining room and living room combined, you'll find you have great freedom in furnishing and decorating any room.

## SOFAS AND CHAIRS

Two of the basic sofas convert to beds at night (just place them next to each other). These are referred to in the text as sofa/beds. There are also other sofas and beds if you prefer to make separate units.

**Do you like a sporty sock sofa? Perhaps an old-fashioned version of the same sofa would be right for your dollhouse. How about the luxury of velvet?**

## Sock Sofa (Color Plate 2)

This can look sporty and modern in stripes or luxurious in prints and solids.

MATERIALS

One pair of teen- or adult-size knee-length tube socks or regular knee socks or two knit fabric rectangles about 9″ X 22″ (depending on the stretchiness of the knit) for back and side sections, and one 9″ X 18″ rectangle for the seat. You'll also need a little fiberfill for stuffing.

STEP-BY-STEP

1. If you are using fabric pieces, fold each piece wrong sides together, sew the seam, and turn. Stuff one sock or fabric piece almost fully with fiberfill and stuff only the middle of the other (figure 2-1).

**Side-back**

**Seat**

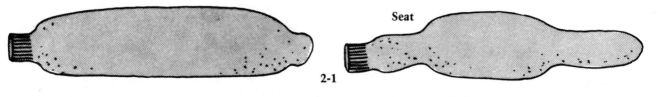

2-1

2. Tuck the ends in and sew in place if necessary (figure 2-2).

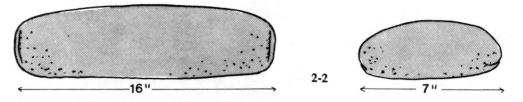

←————— 16″ —————→   2-2   ←——— 7″ ———→

3. Fit the side-back section around the seat. Pin it in place and sew around the top and bottom where the sections meet (figure 2-3).

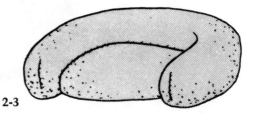

2-3

## Sock or Knit Sofa/Beds (Color Plate 21)

MATERIALS

One pair of knee socks or two knit fabric rectangles about 12" X 18"

STEP-BY-STEP

1. If you are using fabric pieces, fold each piece wrong sides together, sew the seam, and turn. Stuff the middle of fabric tubes or socks with fiberfill (figure 2-4).

2. Tuck the ends in. If they will not stay in place, sew them (figure 2-5).

## Foam Sofa/Beds (Color Plate 4)

MATERIALS

12" square foam pillow form, 2¼" thick
Ball point pen or fine line felt-tip marker
Ruler
Serrated-edge knife

STEP-BY-STEP

1. Measure and mark two 3-dimensional rectangles, 8" X 3¾" X 2¼" on the pillow form. Mark all the way around on front and back in order to get the blocks as even as possible (figure 2-6).

2. To make a guide for cutting, lay the foam piece flat and draw the serrated knife smoothly along the 8" lines on both sides of the piece (figure 2-7). Do not try to cut all the way through at this point.

3. Now stand the block up and saw down using the scored lines as guides. Keep checking back and front to make sure you are cutting straight (figure 2-8).

The leftover foam can be used for dining room chairs and an upholstered sofa (see pages 73 and 41).

*Slipcover/Fitted Sheet (Color Plate 4)*

You can fashion a slipcover for the foam sofa that doubles as a fitted sheet when the sofa is used as a bed. (To use the sofa as a bed simply place the two pieces side by side. The flat sheet, quilt, and comforter are designed to fit over both pieces in this position.)

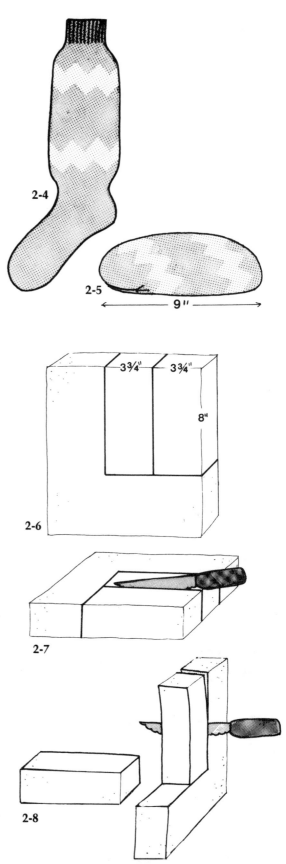

2-4

2-5
9"

2-6
3¾" 3¾"
8"

2-7

2-8

MATERIALS

About ¾ of a yard of 42"–45" fabric is enough to make two slipcovers/fitted sheets, one double flat sheet, two pillow covers, and one or both sides of a comforter or quilt (figure 2-9). (Instructions for the flat sheet, pillow covers, comforter, and quilt begin on page 51.)

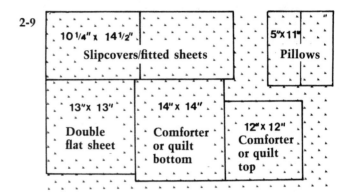

2-9

| 10¼" x 14½"  Slipcovers/fitted sheets | 5"x11"  Pillows |
| --- | --- |
| 13"x 13"  Double flat sheet | 14"x 14"  Comforter or quilt bottom | 12"x 12"  Comforter or quilt top |

SPECIAL HINTS

- Calico, gingham, flannel, or any fabric that catches your fancy will look nice. Flannel and certain other fabrics can shrink when washed, so you may want to preshrink them.
- Measure and mark the dimensions of the linens in pencil on your fabric. Use a T-square to make perfect right angles.

STEP-BY-STEP

1. Make a 3" square template and trace it in each corner of the slipcover fabric piece (you can use one of the 3" pillow patterns on page 45). (Save the extra fabric pieces for napkins and placemats, page 72.) Cut away the corners on the pencil lines (figure 2-10).

2. With right sides together, fold and sew each corner (figure 2-11).

3. Put the slipcover on the sofa wrong side out. Turn the sofa upside down. Turn up the hem and pin it to the right length (figure 2-12).

4. Remove the slipcover from the foam. Turn it right side out and sew the hem. You can add lace or a ruffle if you like.

5. Place the finished slipcover on the sofa right side out (figure 2-13).

2-10

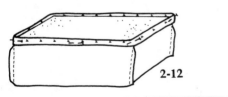

3"

10¼ x 14 ½"

Slipcover/fitted sheet

2-11

2-12

2-13

## Upholstered Sofa (Color Plate 13)

The upholstered sofa is very easy to make yet it gives a deliciously plush and rich look to the living room, especially if you make it in velour.

MATERIALS

⅓ yard velour, velvet, double knit, wool, heavy cotton in plaids, prints—just about any fabric you like will do.

Two 4½" squares, one 4½" X 8" rectangle of corrugated cardboard

12" X 18" piece of quilt batting or some spare fiberfill for wrapping the cardboard

3¾" X 8" X 2¼" piece of foam (follow cutting instructions, page 39)

STEP-BY-STEP

1. Fold an 11" X 20" rectangle of fabric lengthwise, wrong side out, and sew ½" seams along the edges (figure 2-14). Turn right side out.

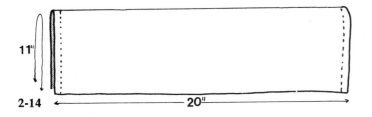

11"

2-14 ←———— 20" ————→

2. Wrap fiberfill evenly around the cardboard pieces (figure 2-15).

3. Insert the wrapped cardboard into the seamed fabric. Tuck the bottom in ½", pin, and hand sew closed (figure 2-16).

4. Fold and sew an 11" X 13" fabric rectangle along the long edge (figure 2-17). Turn it right side out and fit it over the foam piece (figure 2-18). Gather the edges closed (figure 2-19).

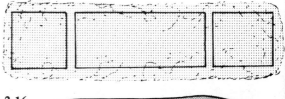

2-15

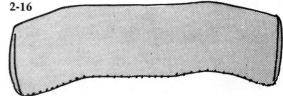

2-16

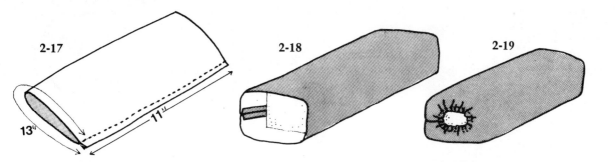

2-17

13"

11"

2-18

2-19

41

5. Fit the back-side piece around the seat. Pin in place and hand sew around the bottom and top where the pieces meet (figure 2-20).

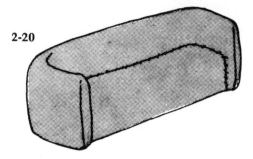

**2-20**

6. Cut two 5″ X 7″ fabric cushion pieces. Sew ¼″ seams in the sides (figure 2-21).

7. Turn, stuff, and tuck in the bottom ½″. Sew it closed (figure 2-22). Place the cushions on the sofa.

**2-21**

7″

5″

**2-22**

2½″

## Sock Chair/Lounge (Color Plate 4)

MATERIALS
One striped stretch sock or other sock (figure 2-23)
Snaps or Velcro fastener

**There are many chair, lounge, and hassock styles to choose from.**

STEP-BY-STEP

1. Turn the sock inside out. Sew the sock about 4″ up from the center of the heel (figure 2-24). (This distance may vary according to the size of the sock you use.)

2. Turn the sock right side out and stuff evenly with fiberfill. Tuck in the cuff. Adjust the shape of the sock chair to your satisfaction, then sew it closed (figures 2-25 a and b).

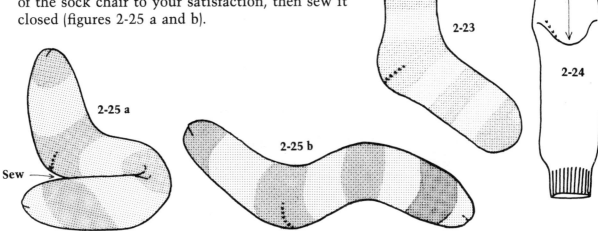

The stuffed sock can be shaped to make a lounge or bed. To make a chair that converts to a lounge, sew on snaps or Velcro fastener at the arrow (figure 2-25a) to hold it together. For a non-converting chair, sew the pieces together at the arrow.

## Sock Hassock (Color Plate 5)

MATERIALS

One sock
A bit of fiberfill for stuffing

STEP-BY-STEP

1. Cut off the top of the sock to the ankle.

2. Place stuffing around the outside of the sock piece.

3. Roll the sock around the stuffing one edge at a time (figure 2-26) so that the edges are enclosed within the hassock (figure 2-27).

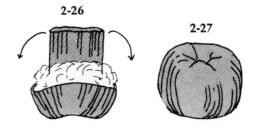

43

## THROW PILLOWS

Throw pillows add a real-life decorator touch to your dollhouse. Place them in the living room or bedroom for a bright accent or use them as comfy floor pillows for the baby dolls to play on. You can be creative in making these very simple pillows by choosing interesting ribbons or fabrics or by drawing your own designs.

### Fancy Ribbon Pillows (Color Plate 17)

These fancy pillows are made from scraps of decorative ribbons and are 2″ to 3″ square, depending on the width of the ribbon. With right sides together sew one seam (figure 2-28). Turn and stuff. Topstitch the other two edges (figure 2-29).

### ❧ Learn-to-Sew: Crayoned Pillows (Color Plate 21)

Crayon coloring is an easy and fun way to make decorative throw pillows. Young children can color their own designs onto the fabric or they can trace the ones given here. Because it is so simple to sew and stuff the pillows, this is a good learning project for them.

2-28     2-29

**Design Patterns for Crayoned Pillows, page 45**

**3″ Square Pattern for Crayoned Pillows**

45

MATERIALS

For each pillow you need a 4″ X 8″ fabric rectangle. The pillows shown in Color Plate 9 were made of white polyester/cotton broadcloth. Pastels work nicely as a background, too, and even scraps of sheets could be used as background fabric. You'll also need crayons and fine line felt-tip pen or laundry pen if you want an outline.

STEP-BY-STEP

1. Trace lightly with a pencil around the 3″ square pattern onto the wrong side of the fabric (figure 2-30). You will be able to see the pattern lines through most white or light colored fabrics.

2. Have the fabric right side up and center the pencilled square over the design. If you like the look of an outline, trace over the lines with a fine line felt-tip pen or laundry pen. Otherwise just color in the design with crayon (figure 2-31).

**2-30**

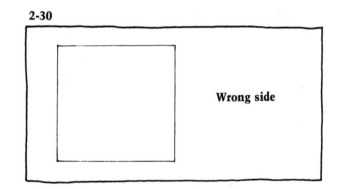

Wrong side

**2-31**

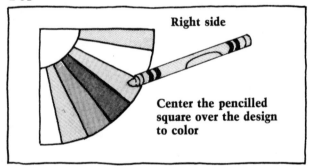

Right side

Center the pencilled square over the design to color

**2-32**

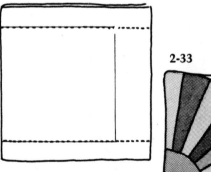

**2-33**

3. Place a scrap of fabric on each side of the pillow fabric to absorb excess color, then iron on a wool-steam setting. This will set the color and prevent it from rubbing off.

4. Fold the pillow piece in half, right sides together. Sew along the two traced lines (figure 2-32). Turn right side out.

5. Tuck the raw edges in, and sew the opening closed (figure 2-33).

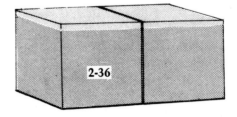
**End tables and storage units.**

## END TABLES AND STORAGE SHELVES

### Double End Table/Storage Shelves (Color Plates 7 and 14)

This is a useful piece of furniture in the dollhouse since it can be used vertically or horizontally as bookshelves, kitchen or clothing shelves, end table, or as any other storage area you might think of.

MATERIALS

    Two 1-quart milk containers
    4″ X 7″ piece of Con-Tact paper for the top
    3″ X 18″ piece of Con-Tact paper for the sides

STEP-BY-STEP

    1. Measure, mark, and cut the two cartons (figure 2-34).

    2. Place the carton pieces together and cover the top with Con-Tact paper (figure 2-35).

    3. Cover the sides (figure 2-36).

You can use these storage units as single cubes or as triple or quadruple units. If you place them vertically, four attached cubes fit snugly under the alcove overhang.

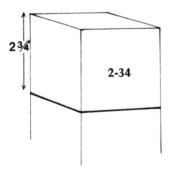

2¾″

2-34

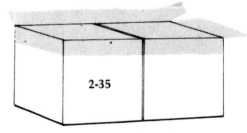

2-35

2-36

# Toy Box/Small Storage Chest

MATERIALS

Quart milk container

8″ X 12″ piece of fabric, paper, or Con-Tact paper

Two ½″ beads

Two 3″ pieces of elastic cord

STEP-BY-STEP

1. Measure 2¾″ up from the bottom of a quart milk container for the sides of the box; measure another 2¾″ for the lid (figure 2-37).

2. Cut out the box and then cover it with fabric, paper, or Con-Tact paper (figure 2-38).

3. Attach the beads on the elastic cord loops to make the closure (see armoire door fastening method, page 58).

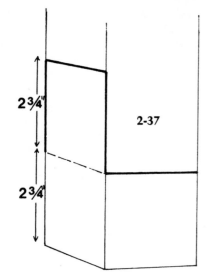

2¾″

2¾″

2-37

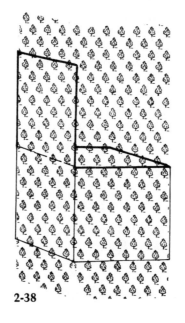

2-38

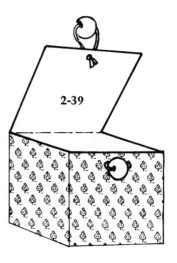

2-39

## Small End Tables (Color Plate 23)

Very stylish end tables can be made from the bottom part of quart milk containers. These tables can be used as school desks, too.

MATERIALS

Quart milk container
4″ square piece of Con-Tact paper for top
3″ X 18″ piece of Con-Tact paper for sides
Ball point pen

STEP-BY-STEP

1. Apply fabric, paper, or Con-Tact paper to the bottom and sides of the milk container (figure 2-40). Mark the cutting lines with a ball point pen (figure 2-41).

2. With scissors cut away the top section of the carton to within ½″ of the marked cutting line. Do not try to cut directly on the line at first.

3. Cut directly on the lines (figure 2-42).

- Make larger tables from half-gallon milk containers. Cut the legs ⅜″ wide.

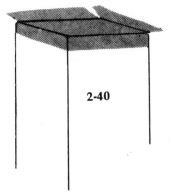

2-40

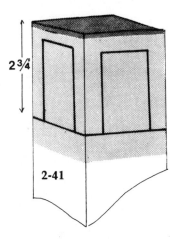

2¾

2-41

2-42

# 3
# Furnishing the Bedroom

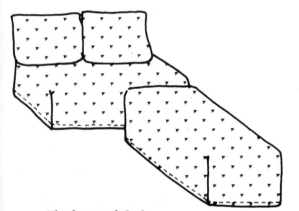

**The foam sofa/bed is a sofa during the day and a double bed at night.**

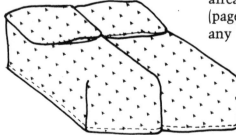

It is now a good time to browse through the Color Plates once more to see how many very different ways there are to furnish and decorate a bedroom. From the same easy furniture pieces you can create several different moods—grown-up sophistication (Color Plate 13), frilly fun (Color Plate 10), fairy tale fantasy (Color Plate 18). You can keep the room simple or make it very fancy, with a lace bedspread and a ruffled bassinet for the baby. You can express your creativity by making a patchwork quilt and other accessories.

## BEDS AND BEDCOVERINGS

The easiest beds to make for the dollhouse are the Sock Sofa/Bed and the Foam Sofa/Bed (page 39). These units function as comfortable sofas during the day and a luxurious double bed by night (see Color Plates 4 and 5). Just place the pieces side by side to form the double bed.

If you have made the Foam Sofa/Bed then you have already made the slipcover that doubles as a fitted sheet (page 39). Following are other linens you can make for any bed style.

## Double Flat Sheet

Use a 13″ X 13″ square of fabric (see layout, page 40). Sew a narrow hem on three sides and a 1″ hem on the remaining side (figure 3-1). The edge with the wide hem is the top of the sheet.

## Pillow

Use a 5″ X 11″ fabric piece (see layout, page 40). Fold the piece in half, right sides together, and sew two ¼″ seams (figure 3-2). Turn and stuff lightly with fiberfill. Tuck the edges in and sew closed by hand (figure 3-3).

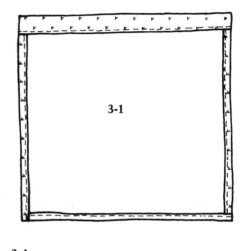

3-1

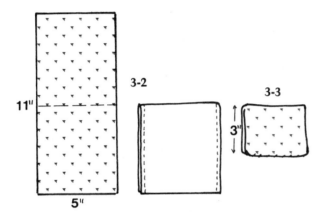

3-2

3-3

11″    5″    3″

## Puffy Comforter (Color Plate 5)

MATERIALS

14″ square of fabric for backing and border (see layout, page 40)

12″ square of fabric for front

Small amount of polyester fiberfill for stuffing

STEP-BY-STEP

1. Place the 14″ square right side down. Then center the thin fluffed layer of polyester batting on the fabric. Place the 12″ square on top, right side out (figure 3-4).

2. Turn up a hem on all edges. Pin and sew (figure 3-5).

3. Sew and tie the layers together with embroidery floss. Place the stitches about 2″ apart or wherever the print of your fabric suggests. To make the stitches, take a small stitch through all layers, then tie a knot and trim the ends to ½″ (figure 3-5).

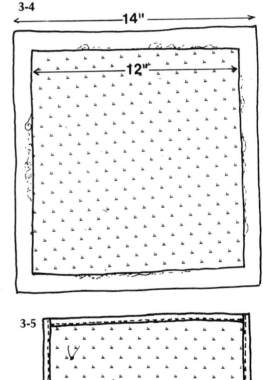

3-4

14″

12″

3-5

## Quilt (Color Plate 8)

You can make a quilt for the double bed out of patterned fabric or you can design your own pattern. Many decorator looks are easy to achieve with ordinary crayons on a solid fabric. You can be as creative and inventive as you like with your own designs; or your child might like to make an original drawing for the quilt top.

**Star of Bethlehem Quilt Pattern, page 53**

*Star of Bethlehem Quilt (Color Plate 8)*

It's also fun—and easy—to make a "patchwork" quilt. (Use the pillow patterns on page 45 for other quilt designs.)

MATERIALS

14" square of fabric for backing and border (see layout, page 40)

12" square of fabric for front

STEP-BY-STEP

1. Trace or photocopy the star pattern from the book first onto a piece of paper, then onto the 12" square fabric piece.

- If you use white or pastel broadcloth you will be able to see the pattern lines through it, so you can simply tape your fabric over the pattern and crayon the design directly onto it (figure 3-6).

2. Turn the fabric after you complete each quarter.

3. Iron the piece to set the color and make it look like a printed pattern and to prevent the crayon from rubbing off. Place pieces of scrap fabric on each side of the design to absorb excess color and iron on a steam-wool setting.

4. Place the 14" fabric square right side down. Center the 12" square over it right side up.

5. Turn up a hem on all edges. Pin and sew.

## Handkerchief Bedspread (Color Plate 19)

Ladies' handkerchiefs are just the right size to use without any alterations. They make the simplest and perhaps prettiest bedcovers. Your child may enjoy doing a crayon drawing on a white hankie.

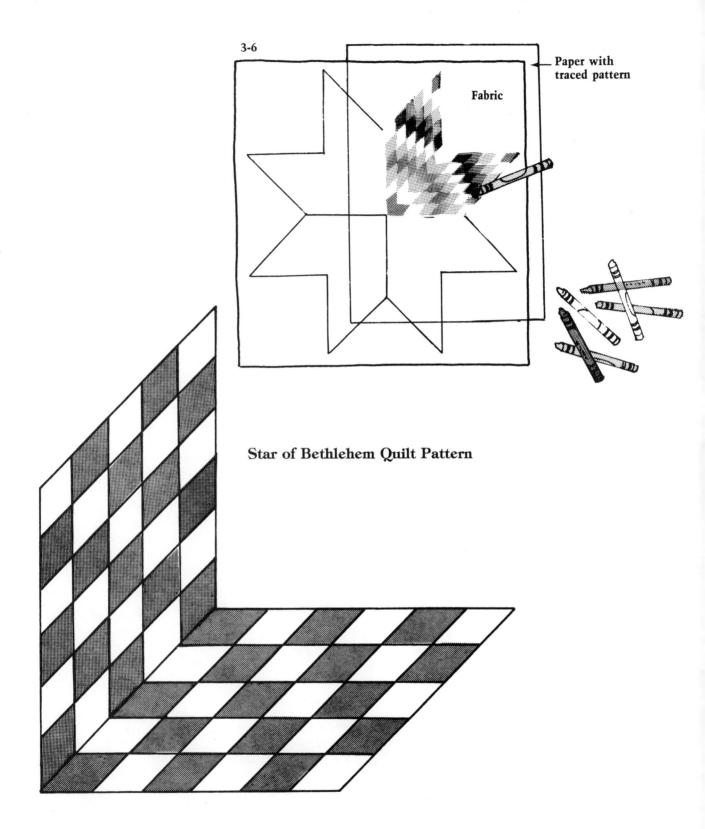

3-6

Paper with traced pattern

Fabric

Star of Bethlehem Quilt Pattern

## Wash Cloth Bedspread

Use the velvety kind as a luxurious, colorful bedspread.

## Lace or Crochet Piece, Antimacassar, or Doily Bedspreads (Color Plate 14)

You may have the perfect piece around your house. If not, they are easy to find in antique and thrift shops. I found some for 25¢. They are certainly elegant additions to the bedroom.

## Canopy Bed (Color Plate 10)

A canopy bed is the dream of many a child. If you can't have one in real life, why not have one in the dollhouse?

MATERIALS

    Two patterned handkerchiefs
    9½" square of corrugated cardboard
    Four empty thread spools
    White glue
    One ¼" X 36" dowel sawed into four 9" lengths
    Cellophane tape
    Glue that works on plastic

STEP-BY-STEP

1. Glue the spools to the corners of the cardboard (figure 3-7).

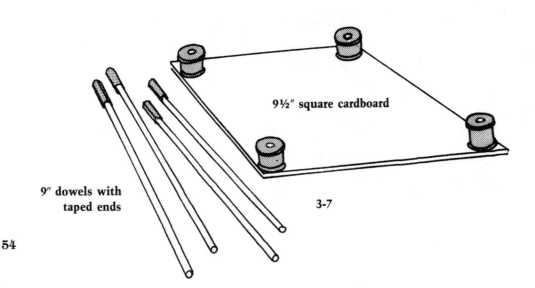

9½" square cardboard

9" dowels with taped ends

3-7

2. Wrap a little tape around one end of each dowel so they will fit into the spools tightly enough to prevent wobbling, but loosely enough to be easily removed (figure 3-7). (If you intend to keep the bed assembled all the time, you can glue the dowels in place.)

3. Place the dowels in the spools and turn the unit over. Center it above two pushed-together foam beds (page 39).

4. Place one handkerchief over the top and one on the bed (figure 3-8).

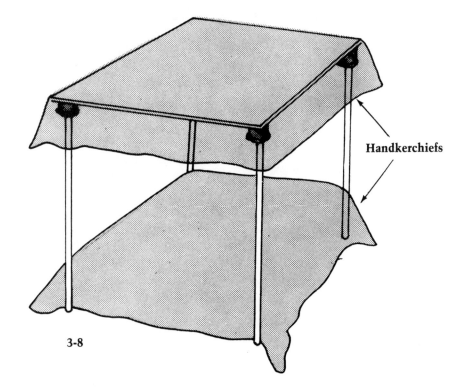

Handkerchiefs

3-8

## CLOSETS

Closets in a dollhouse are special fun. All decorated to match or complement the decor of the room and with doors that can open and close, closets can add beauty and interest to a room. And the inner compartment can satisfy a child's urge to hide things away—in addition, of course, to holding the dolls' clothing and accessories.

**Closets—single and double—can be covered to match or complement your room decor.**

You can make a single closet or a pair of armoires. The doors can be curved around the top or straight-cut. The closets can be covered in fabric or Con-Tact paper, patterned or plain—whatever would make your rooms look the best. You can place a closet anywhere under the alcove overhang.

### Single Closet (Color Plate 8)

MATERIALS

    Half-gallon milk container

    18″ X 10″ fabric or Con-Tact paper piece (you'll need a double layer if your Con-Tact paper is light colored)

    White glue (for fabric only)

    Ball point pen

Sharp scissors to poke holes in milk container
4" long ¼" dowel or a pencil
One or two ½" beads
½" snip of ¾" wide Velcro fastener
Two 3" pieces of elastic cord or string

STEP-BY-STEP: Covering with Fabric (figure 3-9)
1. Place the milk container so that the front faces you.

2. Smooth white glue over the container in a thin even layer one surface at a time. Glue the fabric onto the front first and smooth it down. Then glue the sides, then the back, easing the fabric around. (The top of the closet needs no covering since it is hidden under the overhang.)

3. Clip the fabric to the bottom of the container and fold it under. Glue it in place.

STEP-BY-STEP: Covering with Con-Tact Paper (figure 3-9)
1. Face the spout of the milk container front.

2. Smooth the Con-Tact paper on evenly, first on the front of the container, then around the sides and back. (The top of the closet needs no covering since it is hidden under the overhang.)

3. Clip the Con-Tact paper to the bottom of the container and fold it under. Press it in place.

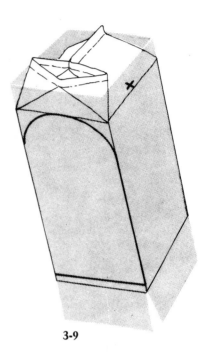

3-9

STEP-BY-STEP: Closet Door
1. Mark the outline of the door with a ball point pen (figure 3-9). Before cutting, place the closet under the overhang to make sure there is enough space for the door to open under the overhang.

2. Cut the straight style door along the top and bottom with an X-Acto knife; cut the curved style door with manicure scissors. Cut the vertical edge of either style with regular scissors.

● If the knife-cut edges are shaggy looking, trim them carefully with manicure scissors.

3. For long-lasting cut edges that won't peel, place a trail of white glue around edge of the door and opening (figure 3-10). Smooth it with your fingers. The glue can be quite thick since it will dry clear.

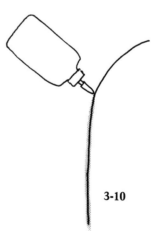

3-10

STEP-BY-STEP: Clothes Rod
1. Cut a small cross with the point of an X-Acto knife on each side of the closet roof. Insert a ¼"

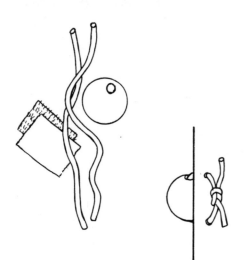

**3-11**

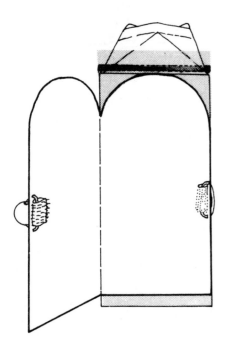

dowel or pencil sawed to the right length through the holes (see figure 3-11).

2. Glue around the dowel and hole to hold the rod in place.

STEP-BY-STEP: Door Fasteners (figure 3-11)

1. Poke two holes about halfway up in the closet door and in the right wall ½" apart and ¼" in from the edge.

2. Thread a bead onto the elastic cord or string. (Elastic cord gives an easier, stronger, tighter tie than string.) Tie the bead to the outside of the door with a square knot.

3. Role the Velcro fastener around the knot and sew it by hand.

4. Make a string or elastic knot on the closet wall. Sew the fuzzy half of the Velcro fastener around the knot.

## Armoires (Color Plate 13)

To make a pair of armoires, cut one closet door as above and the other so that it opens in the opposite direction.

To make door fasteners for the armoires, you'll need two beads and two 6" pieces of elastic cord. Punch the holes in the doors, then string each bead onto an elastic cord. Tie one tight against the right door and the other onto the left door with a loop long enough to go over the other bead.

*Clothes Hangers*

You can bend your own from 9" pipe cleaners or buy a set of plastic hangers for 10" fashion dolls.

## CHESTS (COLOR PLATE 17)

The molded plastic file chest (Color Plate 17) had the right kind of antique wood look and was the right size for a dollhouse chest. Look around in five-and-tens— pretty and unusual file card boxes are available.

## FURNITURE FOR THE BABY

### Playpen

Simply make a fabric pad to fit the bottom of a plastic berry container.

### Hanging Cradle (Color Plate 4)

A sweet hanging cradle can be made from a basket from the five-and-ten. Cut the handle off a 4" long basket and slip a piece of string through the slits (figure 3-15). Follow the upholstered sofa pillow instructions, page 42, to make a mattress. Hang the cradle from paper clip hooks, page 88.

### Bassinet (Color Plate 15)

MATERIALS

    4" basket or 32-ounce white plastic detergent bottle
    ¾ yard of 2¾" wide ruffle
    Two 1¾" high spools
    White glue or airplane glue
    Bunch of party favor flowers

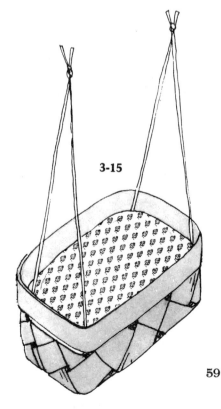

**3-15**

59

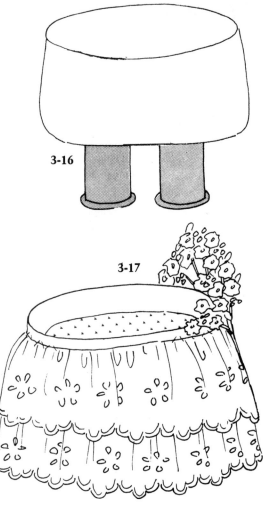

**3-16**

**3-17**

3" Square Pattern,
next page

**3-18**

**3-19**

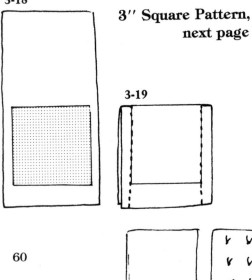

60

**3-20**    **3-21**

1. Mark the detergent container evenly for cutting by propping a pencil 2¼" from the bottom and turning the plastic bottle against it.

2. Use heavy-duty scissors to cut the plastic. (Don't use your good sewing scissors for this.) Trim away the main part of the container to within ½" of the line, then cut right on the line.

3. Glue the two empty spools to the bottom of the bassinet (figure 3-16). (Pieces of wood or anything else you might have that is the right size would do.)

4. Cut two rows of ruffle to the right length for your bassinet bottom and sew side seams. Glue the first row of ruffle to the basket or container so that it touches the floor. Glue the second row around the top. Use white glue for a basket and airplane glue for plastic (figure 3-17).

5. Fan out the bunch of flowers and sew them in place (figure 3-17).

6. Follow the upholstered sofa pillow instructions, page 42, to make a mattress.

## LINENS FOR THE BASSINET AND CRADLE

### Quilt

MATERIALS
4" X 8" piece of fabric (you can crayon your own design or use any light- to medium-weight solid or print)
Polyester fiberfill
Embroidery thread
Lace (optional)

STEP-BY-STEP

1. Pencil around the 3" square pattern onto the wrong side of the fabric (figure 3-18).

2. Fold the fabric right sides together and sew side seams along the pencil line. (figure 3-19). Turn.

3. Stuff the quilt lightly. Tuck the edges in and sew them closed (figure 3-20).

4. Tuft the quilt with embroidery thread (figure 3-21). See page 51 for the technique.

5. If you'd like a very fancy quilt, sew fine gathered lace around the edge (figure 3-23).

## Pillow (Color Plate 15)

STEP-BY-STEP

1. Use a 3″ X 6″ fabric rectangle. Sew the side seams wrong side out (figure 3-22).

2. Turn, stuff, and sew closed.

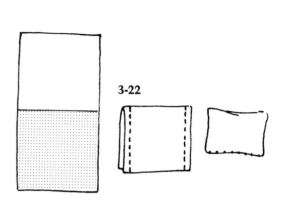

**3-22**

**3-23**

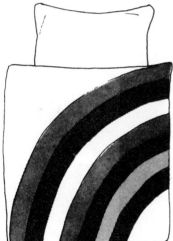

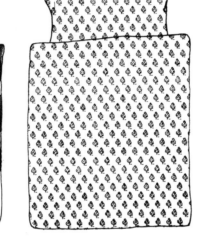

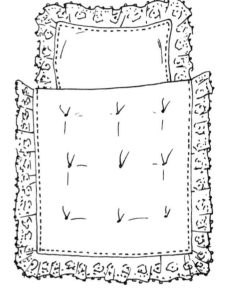

**3″ Square Pattern for the Quilt**

# 4
# The Kitchen

The kitchen in *The Most Wonderful Dollhouse* is another area designed for flexibility and easy room re-arrangement. The kitchen can be a separate room or a part of the living room, as in a studio apartment. In a full kitchen you can place a dining table and chairs, a sink, stove, and refrigerator, cupboards and storage shelves, and you can hang the cooking pots for a decorative touch. In a smaller kitchen you might want to choose only a few of these items. The Color Plates can help you make your decisions.

You can equip your dollhouse kitchen with the latest in modern appliances—sink, stove, oven, refrigerator. Instructions are given here for simple single units and for combination units all made from a half-gallon milk container with a sardine can or soap dish sink. They're easy to make and look realistic. Glance through the photos and drawings to determine which kind you'd like to make.

## COMBINATION KITCHEN UNITS

SPECIAL HINTS
- If you are going to make a sardine can sink, buy a sardine can that opens with a can opener. The key opening kind will peel off the rim that is needed to hold the can in place, so that kind won't work. Make sure there are no sharp edges on the rim.

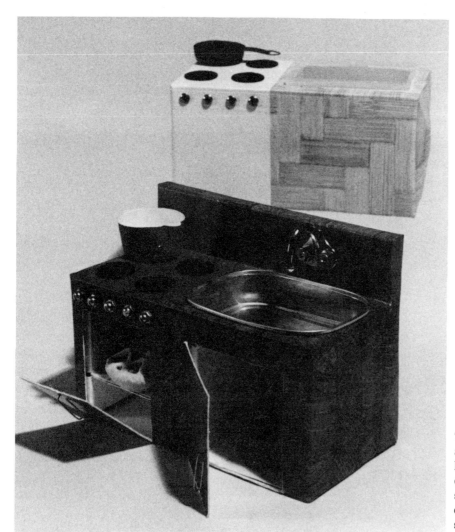

**The simplest kitchen unit has a sink, stove burners, and knobs. The most fully equipped unit has a splashboard, faucet, handles, opening doors, and inside shelves, too.**

- Get the smallest sardine can you can find so the sink does not take up too much room in relation to the stove. A good size is 3⅛″ X 4⅜″.
- Always cut Con-Tact paper to size before peeling off the backing.
- Light colored and white Con-Tact paper require two layers to prevent milk container show-through.

## Simple Kitchen Unit (Color Plate 4)

The simplest kitchen unit has a sink, stove burners, and knobs.

MATERIALS

    Half-gallon milk container
    ½ yard solid color Con-Tact paper
    ½ yard woodgrain Con-Tact paper

Dollhouses

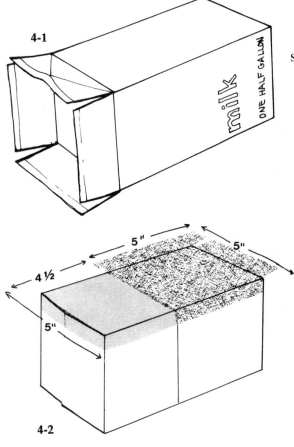

4-1

4-2

Small empty sardine can with rim or bottom of
travelling soap holder with rim
4" square of black felt or paper
Four paper fasteners
Glue that works on plastic

STEP-BY-STEP

1. Open out the top of a half-gallon milk container and clip the corner edges (figure 4-1). Fold the top flat and tape it closed.

2. Set the container on its side and mark a point 5" in from one end. The 5" side is the larger sink portion. If necessary adjust this size to fit your sink.

3. Cut a 4½" X 5" piece of solid color Con-Tact paper (to cover the smaller side) and a 5" X 5" piece of woodgrain (to cover the larger side).

4. Align one piece at a time on the container surface. Clip the Con-Tact paper ends and fold them down (figure 4-2).

5. For the sides, cut an 11½" X 5" piece of solid Con-Tact paper and a 13¼" X 5" piece of woodgrain.

6. Apply to the sides, then clip and fold under the bottom (figure 4-3).

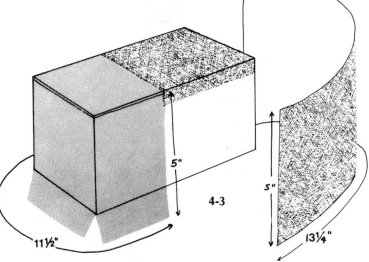

4-3

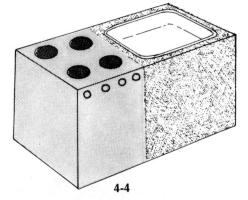

4-4

7. To make four burners, trace around quarters on the black felt or paper. Cut them out then glue them in place with cement or glue that works on the plastic coating of the Con-Tact paper (figure 4-4).

8. The next step is to cut a hole for the sink to fit in. For accurate results, trace your sink bottom onto a piece of paper and cut out along the outline. Then trace this shape onto the milk container.

9. Cut carefully with an X-Acto knife around the outline. The hole must be just the right size to hold the rim and keep the sink from slipping through.

10. For knobs, make small slits in the proper places with the X-Acto knife and glue paper fasteners in place with cement (figure 4-4).

## Kitchen Unit with Opening Doors
## (Color Plate 7)

I found that a single utility hook turned upside down looks pretty much like a faucet. The nuts and bolts, when put through the holes in the hook to attach it to the splashboard, also function as movable handles. The stove bolts are the stove knobs. Bent paper clips or L-hooks and corks are the door handles. Figure 4-5 illustrates all of these elements.

MATERIALS
In addition to the materials for the previous kitchen unit, you will need:

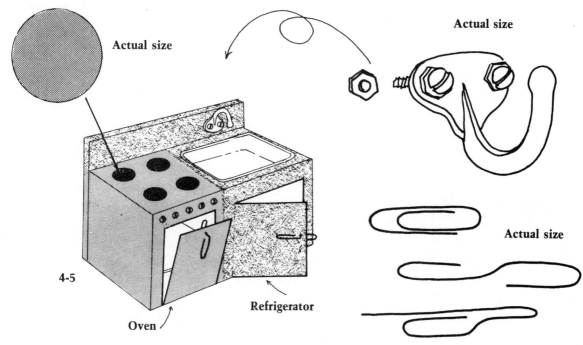

Actual size

Actual size

Actual size

4-5

Oven

Refrigerator

6″ X 8″ piece of cardboard (measurements can vary. See Step 2.)
One utility hook
Two paper clips or two ½″ L-hooks and two small corks
Seven ⁶⁄₃₂″ X ¾″ roundhead stove bolts

STEP-BY-STEP

1. To begin a kitchen unit with opening doors, follow Steps 1 through 4 of the Simple Kitchen Unit, page 63.

2. To make a splashboard, cut two pieces the length of the kitchen unit and high enough for your faucet (the ones shown are 5¼″ X 7¾″) from some leftover cardboard. To get them exactly the same size, cut out the first one and use it as a pattern for the second.

3. Glue the two pieces together.

4. Center a 5″ X 12″ piece of woodgrain Con-Tact paper on top of the splashboard. Clip it as shown and press in place (figure 4-6). Press down the narrow top strip first, then the back, then the front.

5. Glue the splashboard to the back of the unit.

6. Complete the sides and top of the unit by following Steps 5 through 10 of the Simple Kitchen Unit, page 63.

7. To install the faucet, first mark the location of the holes in the utility hook on the splashboard. Make Xs with the X-Acto knife point. Position the hook, insert the bolts, and tighten the nuts on the back.

8. Measure and mark the door dimensions: ¾″ from the top and ½″ from sides for the oven; ¾″ from top and ¾″ from sides for the refrigerator (see figure 4-5). Cut the doors carefully with the X-Acto knife except the refrigerator door bottom; use scissors for that.

9. Finish the edges with glue (see page 57).

10. To fashion a handle with a catch, make a hole in the door with a needle. Bend a paper clip as shown on page 65 and insert it in the hole (figure 4-5). Or, screw an L-hook through the door into a cork (figure 4-7). Turn the cork to work the latch.

**Clip**

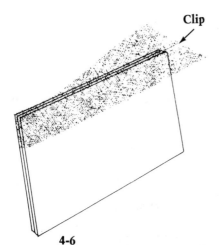

**4-6**

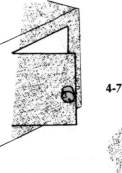 **4-7**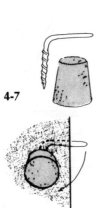

## INDIVIDUAL KITCHEN APPLIANCES

A variation on the kitchen units is to make individual appliances—a refrigerator (figure 4-8), a sink (figure 4-9), or a stove (figure 4-10). To make a sink or a stove only, use a half-gallon milk container and cover it with Con-Tact paper. Generally follow the covering instructions for top, sides, and splashboard on pages 64 and 66, to suit your own needs.

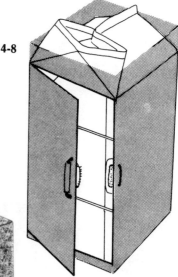

4-8

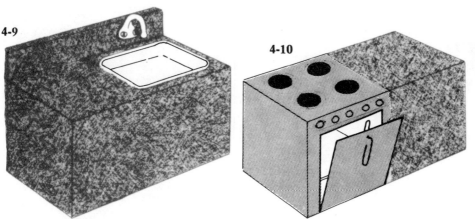

4-9

4-10

### Sink (Color Plate 10)

Use either a sardine can (see page 62) or a larger soap holder. Follow the cutting instructions on page 65.

### Stove (Color Plate 10)

Generally follow the instructions on page 64 but omit the steps for the sink. Follow steps 8 through 10, page 66, for an opening door.

### Refrigerator (Color Plate 14)

Follow instructions for closets, page 56, but make a straight-cut door. You can also make a separate freezer. The refrigerator handle is made from a pipe cleaner, a ½" piece of ¾" Velcro fastener, and a little piece of Con-Tact paper (see figure 4-8).

STEP-BY-STEP: Refrigerator Handle

1. With a needle, make two small holes ¼" from the edge of the door and the side wall.

2. Cut the pipe cleaner in half. Bend each piece and insert one piece through each pair of holes.

**Kitchen appliances are easy to make from milk containers**

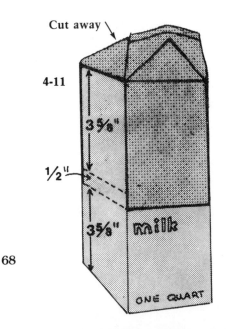

Cut away

4-11

3⅝"

½"

3⅝"  milk

ONE QUART

Twist the ends together. Role the Con-Tact paper around the center sections.

3. Roll and sew a small piece of Velcro fastener around the ends.

*Shelves for Inside the Appliances*

Inside shelves are made from quart milk containers. You'll need one carton for the individual Stove (page 67), two cartons for the Simple Kitchen Unit (page 63), and three for the individual Refrigerator (page 67).

STEP-BY-STEP

1. Mark and cut each carton you'll need (figures 4-11 and 4-12). Dotted lines indicate fold lines.

2. Fold along the fold lines (figure 4-13).

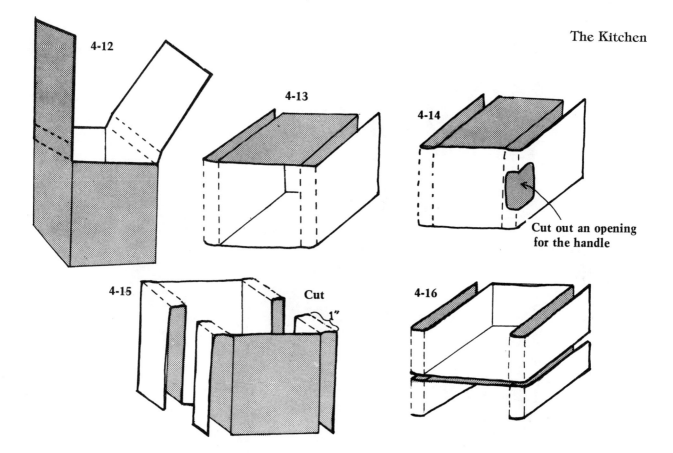

4-12

4-13

4-14

Cut out an opening
for the handle

4-15

Cut

1"

4-16

3. On the middle individual Refrigerator shelf, cut
out a hole to accommodate the handle (figure 4-14).
Stack two shelves inside the Refrigerator, then cut
down a third top shelf to fit (see the photograph,
page 68).

4. For Simple Kitchen Unit and individual Stove
shelves, cut the shelf piece in two, making one
piece 1" wide. (figure 4-15). Turn the pieces around
so that the sides are aligned (figure 4-16).

5. To insert the shelves in the Simple Kitchen
Unit, put the stove shelves in first through the
refrigerator door (which is bigger). Slide them over
to the stove side. Then insert the other set of
shelves.

## TABLES AND TABLE COVERINGS

It's very easy to furnish your dollhouse with tables of
every sort since most of the tables require only one
construction step! You can make a large table for the

**Most kitchen tables require only one construction step.**

kitchen (with matching chairs) and smaller end tables for the bedroom or living room.

Tables in the right scale for the dollhouse and the dolls are about 4″ to 6″ in diameter and 4″ to 4½″ high.

- Turn an 8- or 9-ounce paper cup upside down and fasten a plastic lid from a two-pound coffee can to it with a paper fastener (Color Plate 21). You can add support to the top by placing a smaller plastic lid under the larger one.

- Place a 5″ wooden trivet on an upside-down paper cup. Screw it fast through a washer to the bottom of the cup (Color Plate 7).

- Glue a 5″ trivet to a 4″ high wooden spindle (Color Plate 22) or to a wooden drapery rod end or to a fancy jar or bottle.

- Use half of a photo display block (Color Plate 13). Buy the kind that comes in two halves. Use a half as is or cover it with Con-Tact paper.
- A molded plastic pencil holder makes a very pretty table when turned upside down (Color Plate 17). If you put a trivet on top you can make it a larger table.
- You can make a dining table in the same style as the large end table (page 49), out of a half-gallon milk container. This table would be especially nice with milk container chairs (page 73) as a matching set. The small and large milk container tables can double as school desks (see Color Plate 23).

## Crayon Tablecloth (Color Plate 4)

MATERIALS

8″ square of lightweight gingham. You can use any white or light colored fabric, but gingham makes it particularly easy to fringe the edges.

STEP-BY-STEP

1. You can create interesting crayon designs on yellow, light blue, or pink gingham, or on another fabric you like. Trace the pattern below or design your own.

2. Unravel threads about ¼″ from the fabric edges to make fringe.

### Crayon Tablecloth Design Pattern

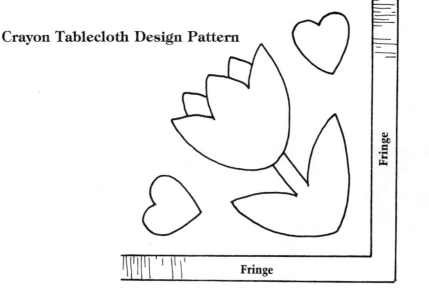

Fringe

Fringe

71

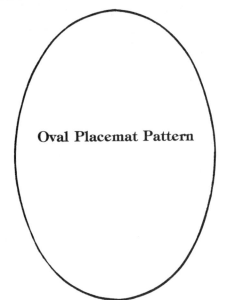

**Oval Placemat Pattern**

### Fabric Tablecloths (Color Plate 14)

Any lightweight fabric can be used. Simply cut it to the right size for your table top. Miniature scarf print fabrics make particularly nice tablecloths.

### ࣌ Learn-to-Fringe: Napkins and Placemats (Color Plate 10)

These easy accessories are just right for children to work on. Simply cut out 3″ square fabric pieces for napkins and 2″ X 3″ pieces for placemats. (You can use the 3″ square pieces you saved from the sheets, page 40.) Gingham is especially easy to use for fringed edges. Unravel the edges about ¼″ to make fringe. You can also make easy oval placemats out of felt. Just trace and cut (see Color Plate 2).

## CHAIRS

The two styles of chairs, Paper Cup and Milk Container, are easy to make, pretty, and versatile. In addition to using them as kitchen chairs, you can use them as side chairs in other rooms (see Color Plate 14). Group them for conversation or place one in an empty corner—wherever the dolls might like to sit comfortably.

### Paper Cup Chairs (Color Plate 21)

Use either 8- or 9-ounce paper cups, an 8″ square scrap of fabric, and a bit of fiberfill.

STEP-BY-STEP

1. Trace the pattern onto a piece of paper, then pencil around the shape onto the cup (figures 4-17 and 4-18). Cutting the cup is easiest with curved manicure scissors.

2. Tie some fiberfill inside an 8″ fabric circle (figure 4-19).

3. Fit this seat into the cup chair (figure 4-20).

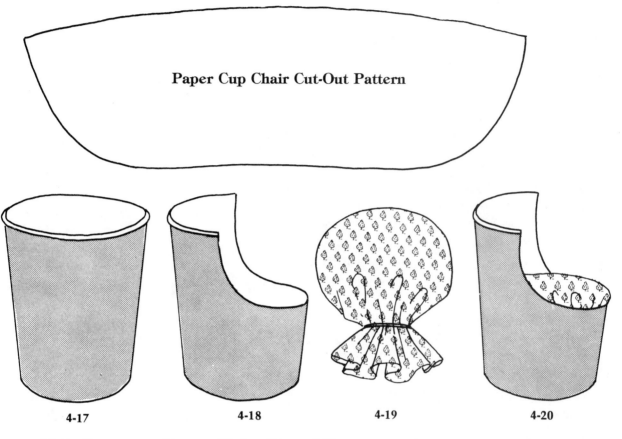

**Paper Cup Chair Cut-Out Pattern**

| 4-17 | 4-18 | 4-19 | 4-20 |

## Milk Container Chairs (Color Plate 22)

MATERIALS

Quart milk container
Ruler
Ball point pen
4″ X 12″ piece of Con-Tact paper
3″ X 9″ piece of Con-Tact paper
2″ X 2¼″ X 2¾″ foam piece (left over from the sofa/beds, page 39)
5″ X 6″ piece of fabric

STEP-BY-STEP

1. Measure and mark with a ruler and ball point pen the front, sides, and back of a quart milk container (figure 4-22). The ink may not show on the container surface, but you should be able to see an indentation.

Making a milk container chair

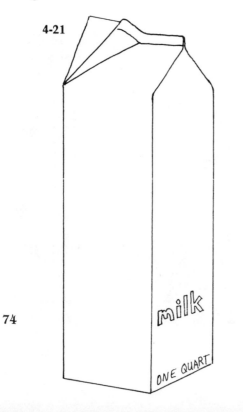

**4-21**

milk

ONE QUART

2. Cut accurately with scissors along the heavy lines in figure 4-22. To make it easier to cut accurately, first cut away the container to within about ½" of the cutting lines. Then cut exactly on the lines.

3. Fold lines are indicated in the illustration by dotted lines. To make folding easier, press along these lines with the ball point pen. Fold along the indentation that results.

4. Cut out a reinforcement piece ¾" X 4" from the leftover carton piece (figure 4-23). Fit it under the chair back (figure 4-24). Tape it in place.

5. Fit the 4" X 12" piece of Con-Tact paper around the bottom part of the chair. Clip and press down (figure 4-25).

6. Fit the 3" X 9" piece around the top section. Clip and press down (figure 4-26).

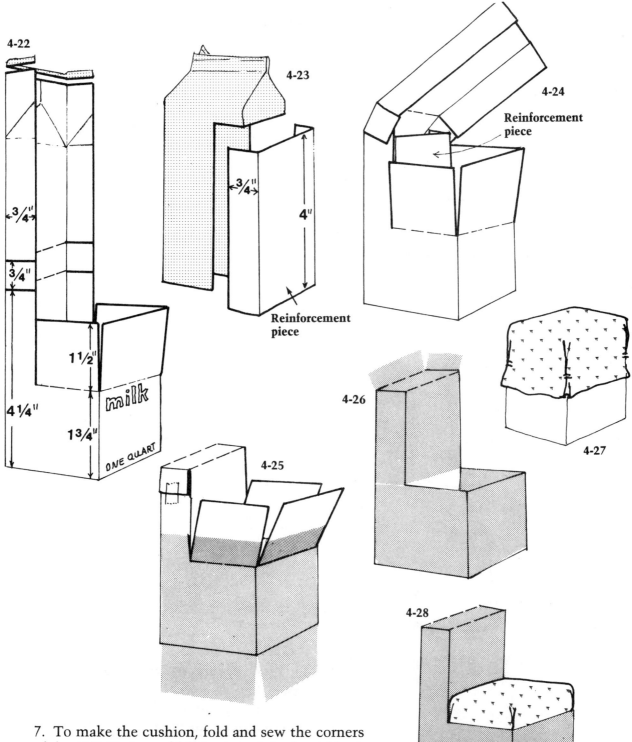

4-22

4-23

4-24

Reinforcement piece

3/4"

3/4"

4"

3/4"

3/4"

1½"

4¼"

1¾"

milk

ONE QUART

Reinforcement piece

4-26

4-27

4-25

4-28

7. To make the cushion, fold and sew the corners of the 5″ X 6″ piece of fabric around the foam block (figure 4-27). Place the cushion inside the chair (figure 4-28).

75

# High Chair (Color Plate 10)

MATERIALS
Two 3-ounce paper cups
Paper fastener
Cardboard scrap
5″ square fabric scrap
Bit of fiberfill
White glue
String

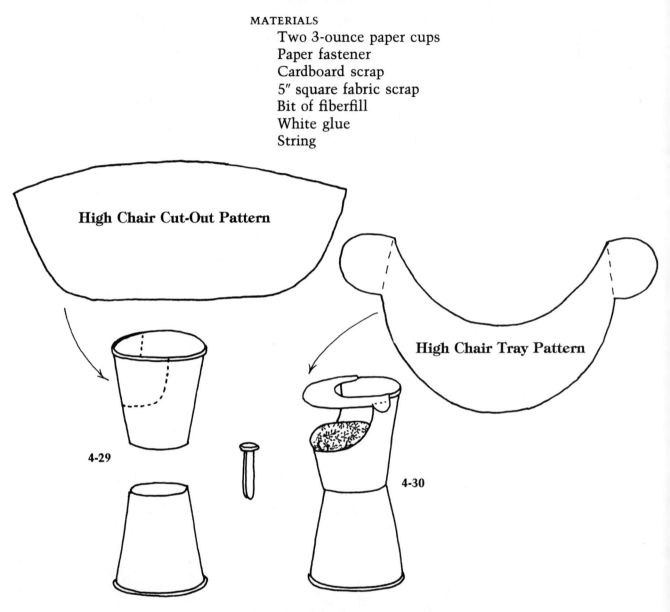

**High Chair Cut-Out Pattern**

**High Chair Tray Pattern**

4-29

4-30

STEP-BY-STEP
1. Mark and cut out one cup (figure 4-29).

2. Attach the two cups bottom to bottom with a paper fastener (figures 4-29 and 4-30).

3. Cut the tray out of the cardboard. Glue or sew it in place (figure 4-30).

4. Stuff a 5″ circle of fabric with fiberfill. Tie it with string and fit it into the seat (figure 4-30).

## DOLL DISHES

Your family of dolls can enjoy their meals on lovely sets of dishes. You can easily make many styles, from "bone china" to everyday-ware. Stack the dishes when they're not in use and store them in a cupboard (see page 47).

### Paper Plates (Color Plates 5 and 11)

The easiest dishes are made from the bottoms of any size paper or foam cup.

First, cut the cup to within ½" of the bottom; then cut it down to the height you want the plates to be. You can leave the dishes plain, paint them, or add press-on stickers or decals for decoration.

## Glue and Bread Clay Dishes (Color Plates 11 and 18)

White glue and bread clay is easy to shape and, after air drying, is surprisingly strong (pieces I have dropped have just bounced instead of breaking), and so it is an excellent material for doll dishes. There are wonderful possibilities for making all sorts of miniatures with this material—beautiful tea sets, toys for the dolls, house accessories—since this clay looks amazingly like porcelain when it is very thin.

SPECIAL HINTS

- Work with small amounts at a time—one slice of bread mixed with one teaspoon or more of white glue.
- Old bread seems to work very well for this dough.
- Use white bread without the crusts for plain white dishes. For brown stoneware, use whole wheat. Add food coloring to produce other colors.
- Use water to add handles and other small parts, making sure they are securely attached.
- The clay can take several days to dry and the items shrink as they dry.

MATERIALS

One slice of bread (enough for three dishes or one teapot)
White glue
3-ounce paper cup (for shaping dishes)

STEP-BY-STEP: Dishes

1. Squeeze about one teaspoon of glue onto the slice of bread and knead them together in your hands.

- This is a messy process at first, so work over spreadout newspapers. After a few minutes of kneading you will have a very workable mixture. Add a drop or two of water if necessary.

2. Roll a ball about 1" in diameter. Press it on waxed paper into a flat circle slightly larger than the paper cup opening.

3. Press the paper cup over the clay to cut out a circle.

4. Peel the clay off the waxed paper. Smooth out any rough edges with water.

5. Put the clay back on the paper better side up. Center the *bottom* of the paper cup over it and press only enough to make an indentation. Turn the rim up.

6. If you like, add decals or painted designs for decoration. To make shiny dishes, apply clear or colored nail polish after the clay is thoroughly dry.

To make smaller plates or saucers use pill bottles or other small round items.

**Dishes, a tea set, and pretend food complete your dollhouse kitchen. Don't forget bones for the dog.**

STEP-BY-STEP: Teapot

1. Mix the dough and follow the Special Hints on page 78.

2. Roll a ball about 1" in diameter for the solid body of the teapot. Make an indentation around the top with a pin (figure 4-31).

3. Roll and shape small strips of dough for the base, spout, and handles (figure 4-31). Make a hole in the spout end. Attach these parts securely with water (figure 4-32).

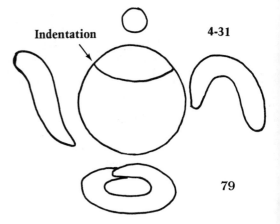

Indentation

4-31

79

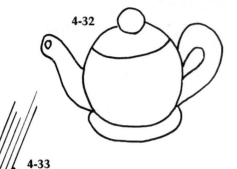
4-32

4-33

STEP-BY-STEP: Cup

1. Mix the dough and follow the Special Hints, page 78.

2. Roll a small ball, then shape the inside of the cup with the blunt end of a ball point pen or a pencil (figure 4-33).

3. Roll a handle and attach it with water.

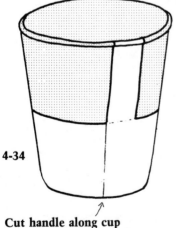

4-34

**Cut handle along cup seam for added strength**

## POTS AND PANS (Color Plates 2 and 11)

MATERIALS

  3-ounce paper cups
  Loop of telephone wire or string
  White glue
  Acrylic paint (water soluble) or leftover latex wall paint
  Old toothbrush (for speckled pots and pans)

STEP-BY-STEP

1. Make the pan any height you want by marking the paper cup at the correct point and cutting (figure 4-34).

2. Make the handle.

80

- For the long-handled saucepan, glue a supporting handle underneath (figure 4-35). Add a small loop of telephone wire or string as a hanger. Glue it under the rolled edge of the cup with plenty of glue.
- For the frying pan, just fold the handle back (figure 4-37). Glue on a loop of wire or string.
- For the two-handled saucepan, bend the handles back (figure 4-38).

3. Paint the pan.

- For solid colored enamel-look pans, just paint the outside and the handle, leaving the inside white.
- To make speckled splatterware, first paint the pan any solid color, then splatter on water soluble acrylic or wall paint with an old toothbrush (figure 4-39). Don't use oil base paint as it is too hard to clean up. Practice this technique on some paper first until you get the feel of it. Put down plenty of newspaper to protect your working surface. Pour a little white paint on the newspaper, then pick up a small amount on the toothbrush. Point the toothbrush toward the pan and brush over the bristles with your finger or a stick.

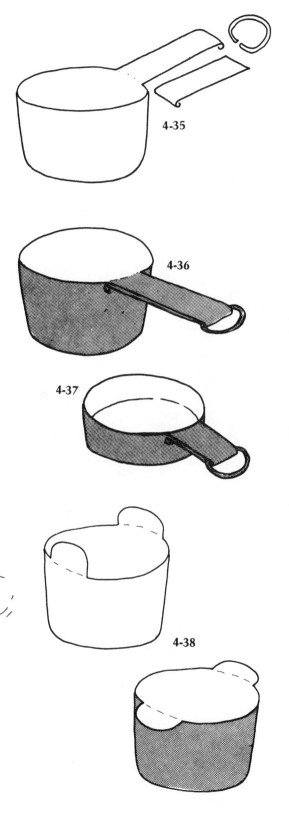

4-35

4-36

4-37

4-38

4-39

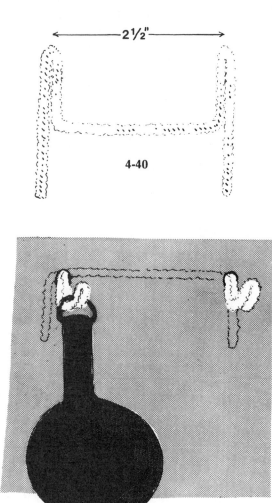

4-40

4-41

## Pipe Cleaner Hooks for Pots and Pans
## (Color Plates 7 and 10)

STEP-BY-STEP

1. Punch holes 2½" apart in the front of the kitchen portion of the alcove overhang with an awl or the point of a small scissors. (See Color Plate 7 for a placement suggestion.)

2. Bend a pipe cleaner to fit the holes (figure 4-40). Then insert the pipe cleaner through the holes from the back.

3. Bend the ends into hook shapes (figure 4-41).

## UTENSILS

You can purchase tiny forks, knives, and spoons in scale with the doll dishes. Spoons can also be made by breaking off the ends of coffee stirrers you can get from fast food restaurants.

## PRETEND FOOD (Color Plates 11 and 19)

What's needed next is some delectable food to put on the pretty plates. What do your dolls like to eat? Oranges? A hamburger? Cherry pie? All of these are easily made from one simple dough recipe.

This dough is made from edible materials. But when it is baked it becomes too hard to eat because of the high salt content. This material is quite strong, but larger pieces can break if they fall several feet onto a hard floor.

The pretend food items are small and look good enough to eat. *Please,* do not make these items for toddlers or any child who likes to put things in his or her mouth. Use your good judgment about which children are old enough to play with pretend food.

MATERIALS

1 cup flour
¼ cup salt
⅓ cup water
Cookie sheet or small aluminum pans

STEP-BY-STEP

1. Preheat the oven to 350°F. Mix the flour and salt together. Add water gradually—variations in

humidity may call for different amounts of water and you don't want to use too much.

2. Working over waxed paper, knead the dough until it is stiff and of an even consistency. It should be stiff enough to hold a shape, but not crumbly.

3. Knead food coloring into small portions of the dough: red for cherries, orange for oranges, a mixture of red, yellow, and blue for hamburgers and hot dogs (heavy on the red for hot dogs). The colors darken when baked.

4. Shape the items.

- Roll little balls for oranges. Flatten the balls to make cookies or buns.

- Make the hamburgers, hot dogs, and buns separately, then squeeze the parts together using a little water to make them stick.

- To make a cherry pie, shape the bottom crust, then fill it with tiny bits of red colored dough. Cut tiny strips of uncolored dough with a knife and weave them across the top of the pie. Use a little water to make the strips stick. To make a blueberry pie, shape the pie, then cut a dough cross in the top and put a little food coloring in the opening.

- To make a jelly roll, press out two flat pieces in different colors. Place one on top of the other. Roll them up and then slice part of the roll.

- Cinnamon or coarse salt is used for the decorative sprinkles. They will stay on permanently if you sprinkle water on your item first and then put on the sprinkles all before baking.

5. If the pieces dry out too much before you get them into the oven, they develop an unattractive white haze. To prevent this either spray them with a mister before baking or put in small batches every few minutes. Check the oven frequently. Very small items—cookies, oranges—can take 5 to 10 minutes; larger ones, 15 minutes or more. Just brown them lightly. They become too fragile if baked very dark. The items can be baked to different shades for variation.

# 5

# Decorating

Decorating the walls of your dollhouse can be as much fun as decorating the walls of your real home, and much less expensive! There are lots of sources for decorative art that can provide just the right accent. And don't forget what a nice touch plants and flowers can be!

## PICTURES FOR THE WALLS

You can buy postcards of real works of art (Color Plate 14) or use the cover of greeting cards you especially like. Your child can make his or her own works of art on index cards (Color Plate 23). You can purchase tiny paintings on canvas for a realistic touch, or you can hang small photographs—portraits of the dolls who live in the house (Color Plate 3) snapshots of your children, pictures of anything you like.

Attach a string to the picture back with lots of glue (figure 5-1) and then place it over a paper clip hook (page 88).

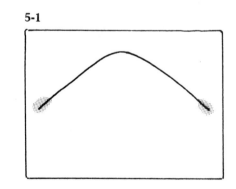

5-1

## HOUSE PLANTS AND POTS

Look through the Color Plates—in nearly every one you'll find plants—peeking out of corners, perking up forgotten places, hanging from the rafters. Plants are a great way to add freshness and greenery to the dollhouse—just as they do in a real house!

Turn the dollhouse into a plant store by displaying your beautiful greenery. The watering cans are shower favors.

## Pots for Artificial or Dried Plants

Plastic plant sprigs or flower bouquets make beautiful house plants when placed in the holes of empty thread spools (Color Plate 18). Toy departments sometimes have bags of wood turnings for sale. These are great for plant pots and other dollhouse items (Color Plate 13). Drill holes in the wood pieces if they don't already have them.

The very realistic pot in Color Plate 7 was made from the Glue and Bread Clay recipe on page 78.

MATERIALS
 One slice of bread is about enough for one small pot.
 White glue

1. Cut off the crust of the bread if you want a pure white pot. Use whole wheat bread for a stoneware look. Mix in yellow, red, and a little blue food coloring for a terra cotta color.

2. Follow the Special Hints and the Glue and Bread Clay recipe on page 78.

3. To make a pot shape, roll the material into a ball, then flatten the base or roll it into a cylinder or pot shape (figure 5-2).

4. Press with a cylindrical object such as a ½″ dowel to make an indentation on top (figure 5-3).

5. Put the artificial plant in place before the pot hardens (figure 5-4).

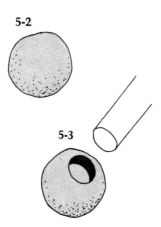

5-2

5-3

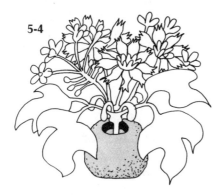

5-4

## Party Favor Flower Bouquets (Color Plate 16)

These tiny velvety flowers come in bouquets of many pretty colors. They are the right size for the dolls to hold. They look especially nice in tiny party favor baskets.

## Dried Plants and Flowers

You can use real dried flowers to make plants for the dollhouse. A branch of dried fern from the florist works well if you break off small branches and group them in the center of a pot. Tie them at the bottom if necessary. You can set any dried flowers in plaster or clay and then place them in a paper cup or plastic bottle top. Tiny dried flower arrangements are lovely in small baskets, pots, or pill bottles packed with moss.

## Live Plants and Flowers

Air ferns are the right size for the dollhouse and need no care at all. If your child would enjoy taking care of small plants, succulents and thornless cacti are easy to care for (Color Plate 21). Place the dollhouse so the plants get enough light.

You can also place tiny bouquets of fresh flowers in water-soaked cotton in pill bottles. (That way the water can't spill.)

## Hanging Plants (Color Plate 13)

If you have empty thread spools with side holes, you can put string right through the holes, and hang plants that way (figure 5-5). For spools with only a center hole, put the string through the hole and tie a very large knot at the bottom that won't slip through. Nice full plants can be hung with no spool at all. Just put the string around the plant itself (you can probably hide it). Hang all of these from paper clip hooks, below.

*Paper Clip Hooks*

Regular size paper clips are fine for most purposes. You may want to use larger ones for hanging certain plants.

To hang most plants and pictures, simply bend the paper clip and hange it over the wall (figure 5-6). Place the plant on the hook (figure 5-7).

To hang a paper clip hook in the alcove, straighten the bottom of the hook and punch it through the alcove top at the chosen location (figure 5-8). Rebend the bottom of the hook after the hook is in place. Place a plant on it.

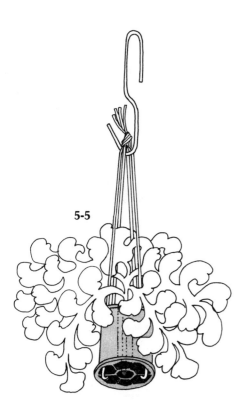

5-5

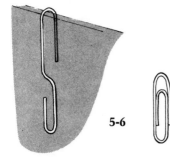

5-6

5-7

5-8

## AN INTRODUCTION TO FLOOR PLANS

*The Most Wonderful Dollhouse* was designed so that children could have fun rearranging the furniture, closets, and appliances. This introduction to floor plans can help them learn even more about furniture arrangement and space relationships.

If you were looking down on a room directly from above you would see the top outline of the room and the furnishings in it. This is what a floor plan represents—a view from above with the sizes of the room and furnishings all in true proportion to one another.

The floor plan presented here is in one-quarter scale. This means that 1″ in the floor plan equals 4″ in the actual dollhouse. You will find here the outlines for the room, closet, appliances, and major furniture pieces. If you want to make additional furniture pieces for the floor plan, just make them one quarter of their actual size.

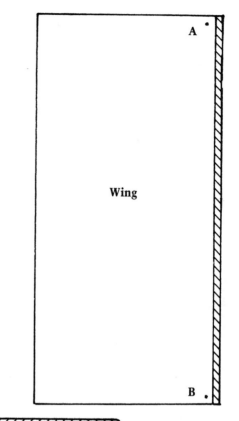

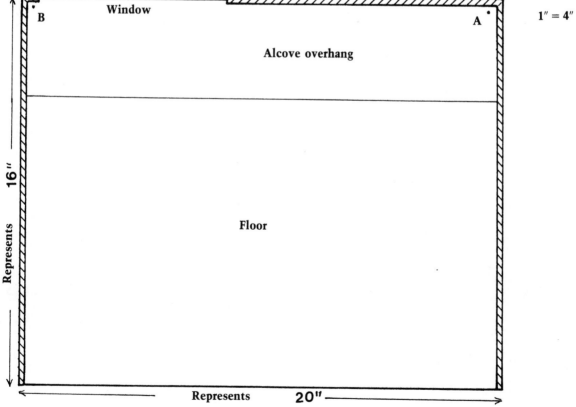

89

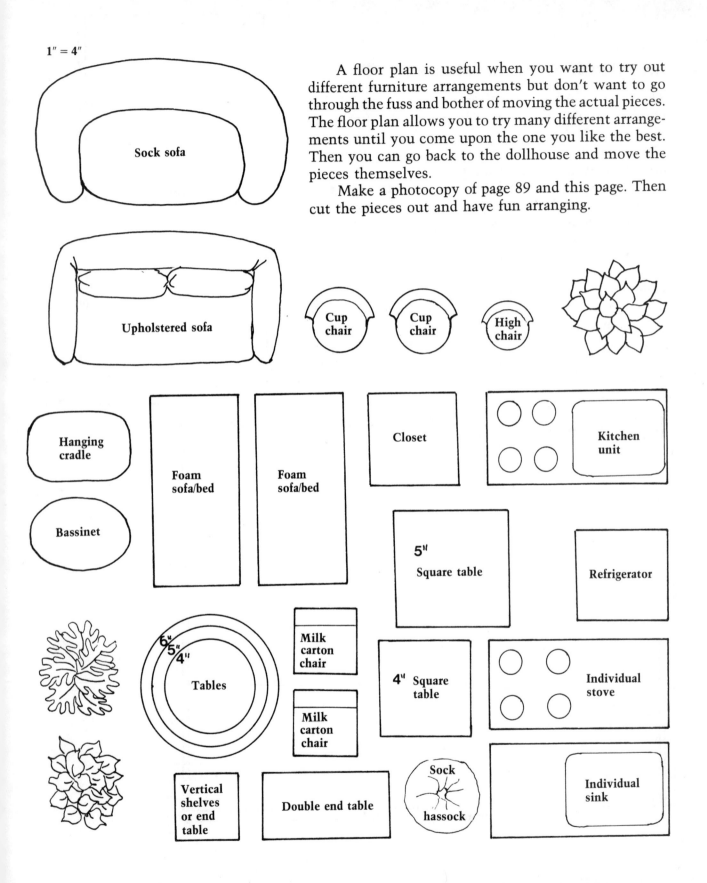

1″ = 4″

Sock sofa

A floor plan is useful when you want to try out different furniture arrangements but don't want to go through the fuss and bother of moving the actual pieces. The floor plan allows you to try many different arrangements until you come upon the one you like the best. Then you can go back to the dollhouse and move the pieces themselves.

Make a photocopy of page 89 and this page. Then cut the pieces out and have fun arranging.

Upholstered sofa

Cup chair

Cup chair

High chair

Hanging cradle

Foam sofa/bed

Foam sofa/bed

Closet

Kitchen unit

Bassinet

5″ Square table

Refrigerator

Milk carton chair

6″ 5″ 4″ Tables

4″ Square table

Individual stove

Milk carton chair

Vertical shelves or end table

Double end table

Sock hassock

Individual sink

# part two

# DOLLS AND THEIR CLOTHING

# 6
# Making the Dolls

The doll families that live in these houses are cute, lovable, and big enough to dress and pose and play with. They are 9″ tall and fit confortably on all the chairs, sofas, and beds you can make for the house. The baby dolls are 4″ tall.

There are two types of dolls—predressed and dressable. Both are the same size, but the predressed dolls are simpler to make and are perhaps better for younger children to play with. The dressable dolls have clothing that can be changed and more detail in their hair and features. Both types of dolls have hand snaps. With hands snapped together the dolls can hold bouquets or hold their babies in their arms. The dolls can hold hands with each other, too.

To stand the girl doll for play or display, put an empty bathroom tissue roll under her skirt. If you fashion fancy clothing for them you can have charming collector's costumed dolls.

## WHICH KIND SHOULD I MAKE?

The predressed dolls are exceptionally quick and easy to make. As you can see from the photo on page 96 they consist of a head and torso piece with very simple clothing sewn on. Although the dolls' basic clothing is not changeable, they have some easy-to-make-and-change garments: two vests, hats, and an apron. Many of these extras can be made by children

The easy predressed dolls are perfect for toddlers. You can make a dollhouse without walls for them by spreading out a handkerchief rug and making a few simple pieces of furniture.

as learn-to-sew projects. The dolls' floppy unstuffed cloth limbs make them very easy for young children to pose.

A dressable doll can be a school girl one minute and a princess the next. All it takes is a change from a sporty knit dress made from a sock to a fairy tale gown made from a handkerchief.

The head and torso piece of the dressable dolls is the same as that of the predressed dolls; arms, legs, and embroidery floss hair make the difference. Linked pipe cleaner joints in the arms and legs, which are designed for safety and long wear, allow the dolls to assume realistic poses. They also give the arms and legs the stiffness they need to go easily through pants legs and long sleeves. In addition to being able to hold things in their clasped arms, the dressable dolls can hold small items such as pencils, spoons, and the stem of a flower in their folded hands.

A wonderful wardrobe can be made of scraps, throwaways, and inexpensive materials. You won't believe how easy it is to make beautiful, sophisticated clothes with all-in-one-piece patterns. Some of these use a white glue edge-finishing method for sturdy non-ravelling edges without hemming. A special learn-to-sew dress can provide a child's introduction to sewing. The dressable dolls also can wear the learn-to-sew vests, hat, and apron.

## FABRIC FOR THE DOLLS

The dolls you make can have any shade of skin you prefer. (The ones in the book are made from a woven cotton fabric called earth cloth whose weight is slightly heavier than Indian head cotton.) It can be difficult to find the right color. Unbleached muslin, pink, tan, or brown fabrics make nice-looking dolls. If you decide to dye a fabric to get the color you want, remember that while it is wet the fabric will be darker. Always do a test sample.

The fabric should have some body to it—although I used woven fabric, a double knit would also work well. Avoid too-thin, ravelly fabrics. The more important consideration is the color, however, so if you find the perfect color in a thin fabric, by all means try it out.

You might want to spray on a fabric protector to prevent soiling. You can wash or dry-clean the dolls, but unless you use acrylic paint you'll have to redraw the faces of the predressed dolls after doing so (the ink will come out).

SPECIAL HINTS ON THE DOLLS AND THEIR CLOTHING

- You can sew any project by hand or machine. When one method is better than the other, it says so in the instructions.
- In general, light- to medium-weight fabrics— calicos, ginghams, etc.—will work best for the clothing.
- Occasionally ¼" snaps are specified. This size is strong enough to take wear and tear. You might want to use smaller snaps for articles of clothing.
- Sewing lines appear on the patterns.

## PREDRESSED DOLL (Color Plate 1)

MATERIALS

7" square of medium-weight flesh colored fabric
Scraps of fabric for clothing (see patterns, pages 122, 123, and 125)
Polyester fiberfill stuffing
Sewing thread to match fabric
Buttonhole twist (optional, for sewing on the snaps and arms by hand and tying the neck)
Laundry or ball point pen, or fine line marker
Felt-tip marker, crayon, or watered-down acrylic paint
¼" snaps (two for each doll)
Pink crayon for rosy cheeks (optional)

STEP-BY-STEP: Head and Torso Piece

1. Place the patterns on the straight grain of the fabric. Poke through the pattern dots with a pencil to mark the facial feature dots on the right side of the front piece (figure 6-1). Make the marks very faint so that they won't show after the face is drawn.

**Use Boy Torso Pattern only, page 129**

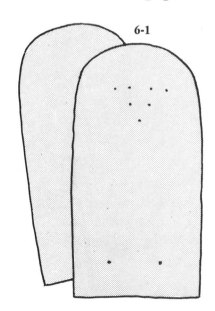

6-1

95

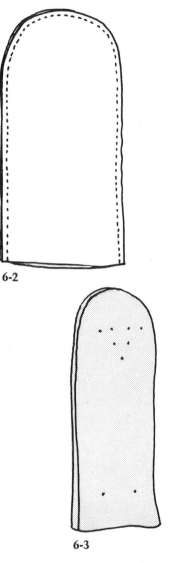

**6-2**

**6-3**

**6-4**

2. Sew the back to the front, right sides together (figure 6-2). Turn (figure 6-3).

3. Stuff, pushing in the stuffing tightly.

4. Tuck the excess fabric into the front side and sew (figure 6-4).

5. Wrap and tie tightly at the neck dot to form the neck, using two thicknesses of buttonhole twist figure 6-4). You can also use string, embroidery floss, or thread.

COLOR PLATE 1
The Predressed Dolls are the simplest dolls to make (page 95). They're soft and
huggable, so they're just right for even the littlest hands. They can hold hands and
be placed in real-life poses.

COLOR PLATE 2
The Predressed Dolls are at home in this basic one-room dollhouse. The house is cozy in warm Victorian browns. The soft stuffed sock furniture (page 38) is perfect for younger children to play with. The room-size rug is a pretty scarf (page 22).

COLOR PLATE 3
The same basic house takes on a different tone when the sofa and chairs are made from brightly striped socks. The simple table has only one construction step (page 70).

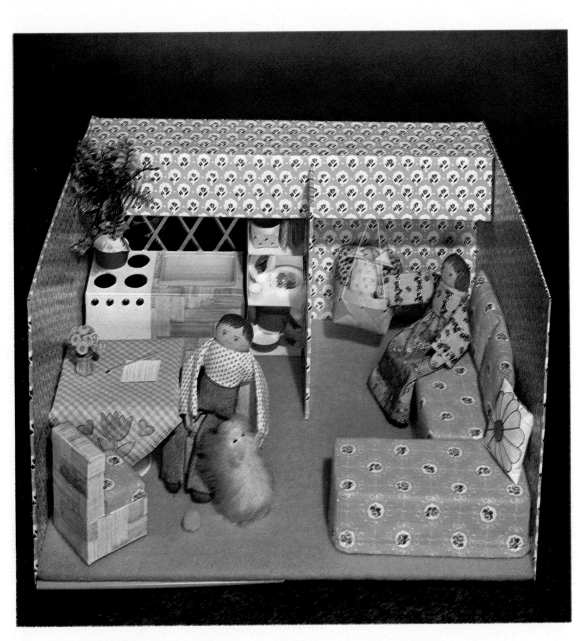

COLOR PLATE 4
This cheery studio apartment features color-coordinated walls, floors, and furnishings. Your child might like to color a tablecloth (page 71). The sofas are easy to make and have removable covers (page 39).

COLOR PLATE 5

The same yellow dollhouse has a completely different look when one wing is opened out. The pretty garden is lush and expansive (page 34). A piece of indoor-outdoor carpet makes a beautiful lawn as well as a comfortable place for children to sit.

COLOR PLATE 6
Here are the Dressable Dolls (page 127). They can be posed realistically with their jointed arms and legs. Their outfits are made from children's socks (page 155) and have the look of expensive knits. Their other changeable outfits are simple to sew, too.

COLOR PLATE 7
This basic blue house with an open wing is an inviting setting for daytime
activities — reading, making meals, and playing with the baby. The flowers and
plants (page 85) provide a fresh, wholesome atmosphere.

COLOR PLATE 8
At night the same house is transformed! Just move the two sofas together to make a comfy double bed. The Star of Bethlehem quilt (page 52) adds a special touch to the room.

COLOR PLATE 9
The materials for the Star of Bethlehem quilt and for the pillows (page 44), tote bag
(page 170), tablecloth (page 71), and apron (page 166) couldn't be simpler—scraps of
fabric, crayons, and the patterns in the book!

COLOR PLATE 10

This fancy two-story house is the delight of many a child. It's made from the same simple design as the white house in Color Plates 2 and 3. Even the canopy bed (page 54) and the bassinet (page 59) are easily made from household items.

COLOR PLATE 11
The Dressable Dolls go on a picnic and bring their pet dog (page 196) along! The recipe for the appetizing pretend food appears on page 82. Making the dishes (page 77) and pots and pans (page 80) are part of the fun, too.

COLOR PLATE 12
The happy couple gets married! The groom's outfit (page 179) and the bride's gown (page 181) are traditional and romantic, but you'll never guess how easy they are to make.

COLOR PLATE 13
All you need to do to transform the basic house into this sophisticated two-story dollhouse is use different materials for the walls, floors, and furnishings. The removable roof (page 30) is an elegant option.

COLOR PLATE 14

For some children having a three-story town house is a dream come true. You can make this one easily and inexpensively. The house has a fully equipped kitchen (page 62), an upholstered sofa (page 41), and lacy coverings for the bed (page 54) and window (page 26). The doghouse (page 34) is another fun-to-play-with addition. It can be used with any dollhouse.

COLOR PLATE 15
Here you can see the lovely details of the bassinet (page 59) and the baby doll's handkerchief dress (page 158).

COLOR PLATE 16
These fanciful handkerchief gowns (page 187) inspire the imagination. Your child will have fun inventing dress-up occasions and fairy tale settings for the dolls to wear them in—like a Prince and Princess's castle, next page.

COLOR PLATE 17
The Prince and Princess enjoy the luxurious comfort of their fairy tale castle chamber. The ribbon pillows (page 44) and wood-look chests (page 58) help to provide the old-world feeling.

COLOR PLATE 18
In a nearby castle the table is set for tea (page 79). This castle chamber is decorated
with handkerchief tapestries.

114

COLOR PLATE 19
At night in the castle the Princess cuddles with her pet cat (page 198).

COLOR PLATE 20
The lovable Bear family—Mama, Papa, and the twin cubs—pose for a portrait (page 191).

COLOR PLATE 21
The simple Bear house is just right for younger children to play with. The hanging cradle (page59), sock sofa/beds (page 39), and paper cup chairs (page 72) are all quick to make and hard to break.

117

COLOR PLATE 22
The Bears are at home in their pretty red and white cottage. Papa reads a book (page
171) to the children while Mama knits (page 171).

COLOR PLATE 23
The simple Bear house (Color Plate 21) converts to a school with the perfect atmosphere for learning. The students love what they learn from their books and they're proud of their artwork hanging on the wall (page 85). When they need a rest they look out the window at the view (page 26).

COLOR PLATE 24

Ah! Everyone needs a vacation and the Bears know just how to spend theirs. Mama relaxes on a sock lounge (page 42) while Papa fishes (page 193). The twins take turns floating in the inner tube (page 193).

You'll be surprised how much personality can come through in just a few lines.

1. Connect the dots to make the lower line of the eye using a fine line marker, ball point pen, laundry pen, or watered-down acrylic paint with a fine brush or pen. Refer to the photographs and draw the rest of the eye.

- If you'd like to make freckles and rosy cheeks, see page 134.

- You can make a regular front and back, face on one side, hair on the other, or an awake/asleep doll.

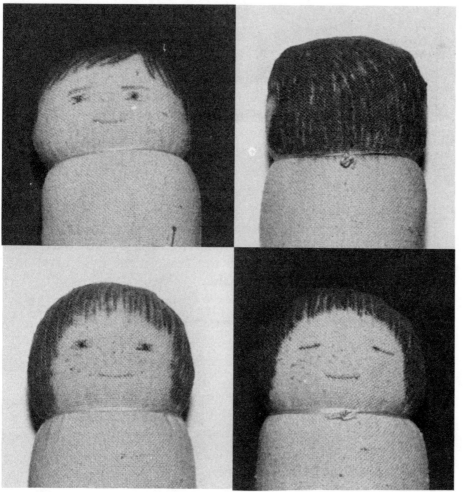

**Regular front and back**

**Awake/asleep**

**Shirt/Blouse Pattern**

Cut 2

2. Use a felt-tip marker, crayon, or watered-down acrylic paint for the hair.

- If you would prefer to embroider faces and hair, see pages 133 and 135.

STEP-BY-STEP: Shirt/Blouse and Hands for a Boy or Girl Doll

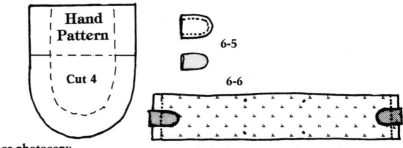

**Hand Pattern**

Cut 4

6-5

6-6

Trace or photocopy these patterns.

1. Sew and turn the hands (figure 6-5).

2. Mark and cut the shirt/blouse front and back. Sew the hands to the front only of the shirt/blouse (figure 6-6).

3. Sew the back and front together, right sides together (figure 6-7).

4. Turn. Hand stitch to close the sleeve opening (figure 6-8).

5. Sew on the hand snaps placing the half with the hole on the right hand (figure 6-9). Make sure you put the half with the hole on the right hand on every doll you make.

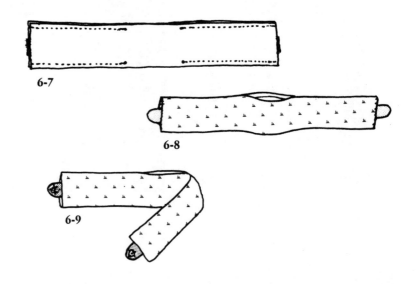

6-7

6-8

6-9

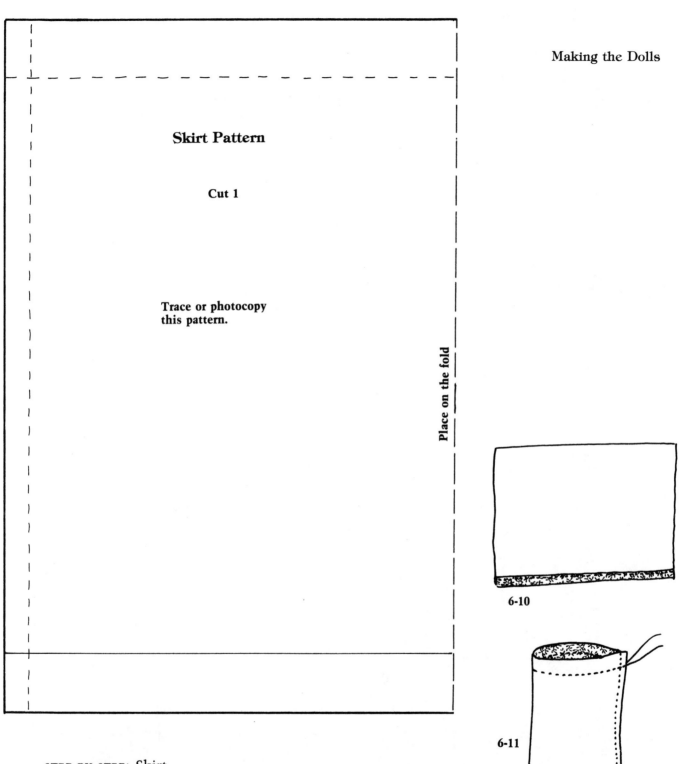

**Skirt Pattern**

**Cut 1**

**Trace or photocopy
this pattern.**

Place on the fold

**6-10**

**6-11**

STEP-BY-STEP: Skirt
1. Sew the bottom hem (figure 6-10).
2. Sew the side seam and gather the waist with small running stitches (figure 6-11).

123

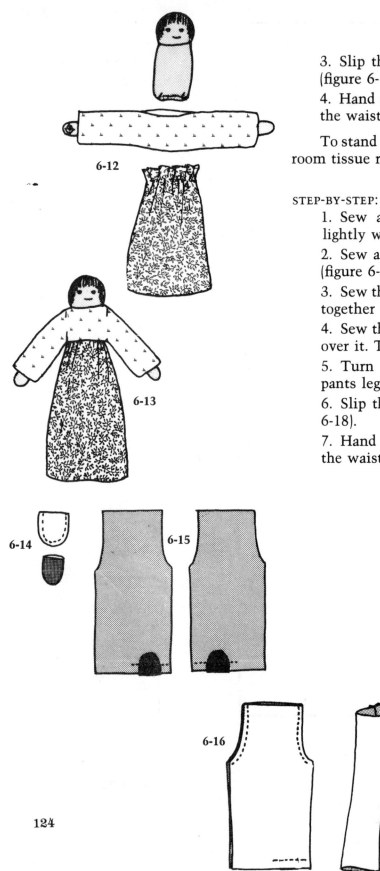

3. Slip the blouse and skirt onto the torso piece (figure 6-12).

4. Hand stitch the skirt and blouse to the doll at the waist and neck (figure 6-13).

To stand the doll, place the torso in an empty bathroom tissue roll under the skirt.

STEP-BY-STEP: Pants

1. Sew and turn the shoes (figure 6-14). Stuff lightly with fiberfill.

2. Sew a shoe to the right side of each pants leg (figure 6-15).

3. Sew the front and back center seams right sides together (figure 6-16).

4. Sew the leg seams only to the center seam, not over it. Then backstitch (figure 6-17).

5. Turn the pants, and hand stitch to close the pants legs at the shoes (figure 6-18).

6. Slip the shirt and pants onto the torso (figure 6-18).

7. Hand stitch the pants and shirt to the doll at the waist and neck.

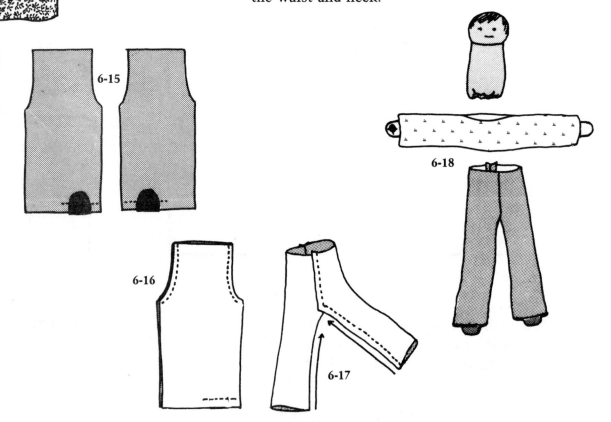

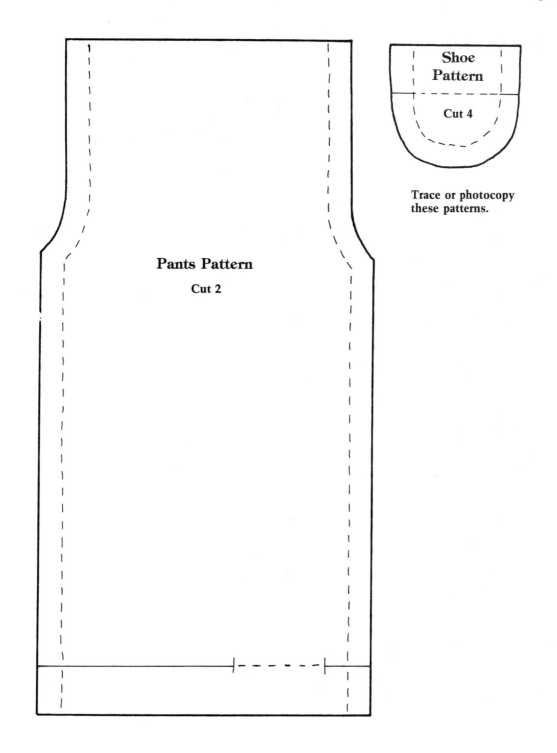

**Shoe Pattern**

Cut 4

Trace or photocopy these patterns.

**Pants Pattern**

Cut 2

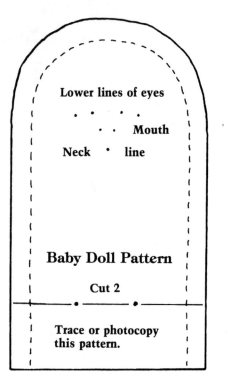

Lower lines of eyes

$\cdot \ \cdot \ \cdot \ \cdot$

$\cdot \ \cdot$ **Mouth**

**Neck** $\cdot$ **line**

**Baby Doll Pattern**

**Cut 2**

$\cdot \text{—} \cdot$

**Trace or photocopy
this pattern.**

## PREDRESSED BABY DOLL

**STEP-BY-STEP**

1. Cut out the fabric on the straight grain; mark the dots for the facial features.

2. Place front and back right sides together and sew around the edge.

3. Turn and stuff.

4. Tuck the excess fabric into the front side and sew closed. Tie the neck (figure 6-19).

5. Make the face and hair as for the grown-up dolls (see page 121).

## Bunting for the Predressed Baby Doll

**STEP-BY-STEP**

1. Use the pattern to cut a square of cotton flannel or other fabric placing the top edge along the selvage.

**To mark dots, poke through traced pattern with a sharp pencil.**

6-19

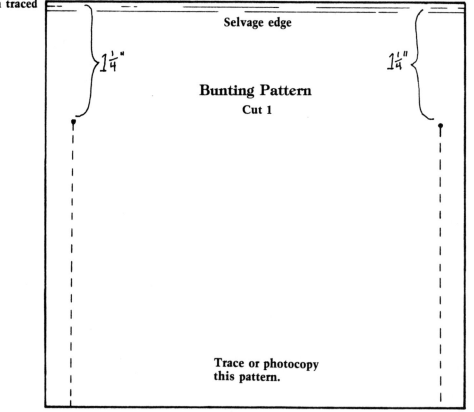

Selvage edge

$1\frac{1}{4}"$        $1\frac{1}{4}"$

**Bunting Pattern**

**Cut 1**

**Trace or photocopy
this pattern.**

2. Hand sew a narrow seam starting at the top and going down 1″ on both sides (figure 6-20).

3. Fold the piece right sides together and sew a ¼″ seam starting 1¼″ from the top (figure 6-21).

4. Place the seam at the center and sew across the bottom ¼″ from the edge (figure 6-22).

5. Turn right side out. Put in the baby doll. Sew at the neck seam to hold the baby in place (figure 6-23).

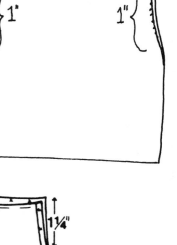

6-20

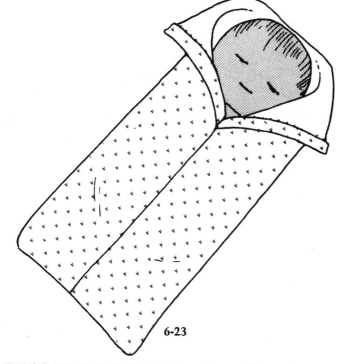

6-23

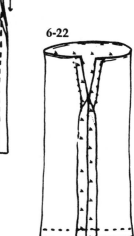

6-21

6-22

## DRESSABLE DOLL (Color Plate 6)

MATERIALS

⅜ yard medium-weight flesh colored fabric

Polyester fiberfill stuffing

Sewing thread to match fabric

Buttonhole twist (optional, for sewing on the arms and snaps by hand and for tying the neck)

Ten 6″ long standard pipe cleaners

Plastic tape, ¾″ wide

Acrylic paint for shoes

Colored sewing thread for face

Embroidery floss for hair (amounts vary according to hair style)

Pink crayon for rosy cheeks

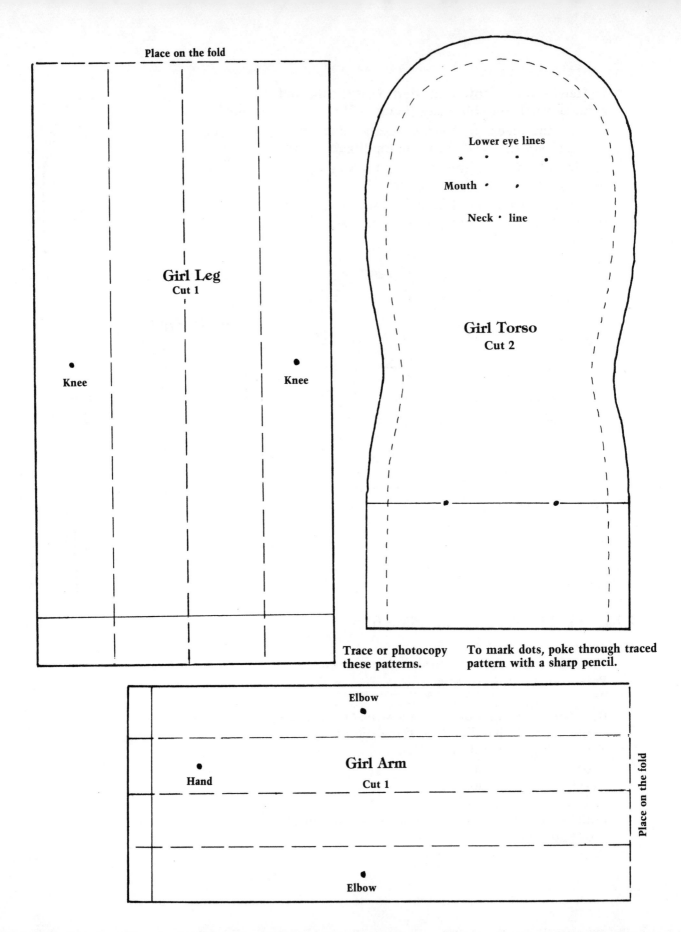

Place on the fold

Girl Leg
Cut 1

Knee
Knee

Lower eye lines

Mouth

Neck · line

Girl Torso
Cut 2

Trace or photocopy
these patterns.

To mark dots, poke through traced
pattern with a sharp pencil.

Elbow

Hand

Girl Arm
Cut 1

Place on the fold

Elbow

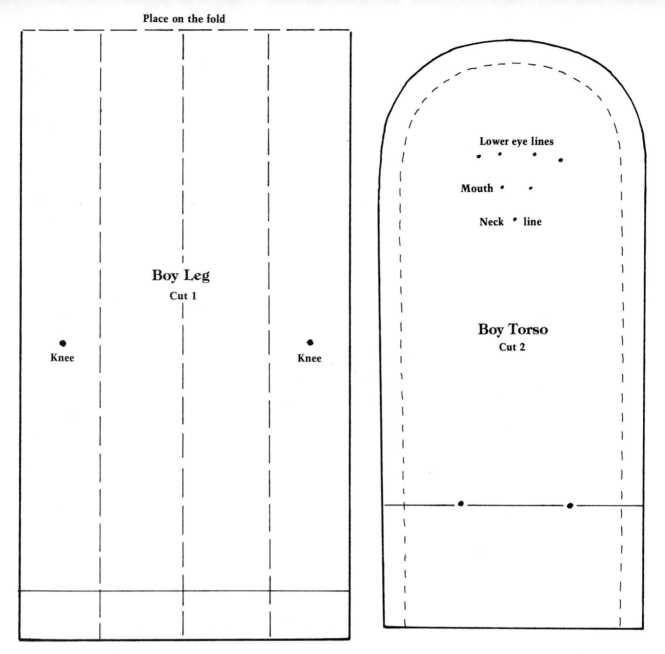

**Place on the fold**

**Boy Leg**
Cut 1

Knee

Knee

**Lower eye lines**

**Mouth**

**Neck** line

**Boy Torso**
Cut 2

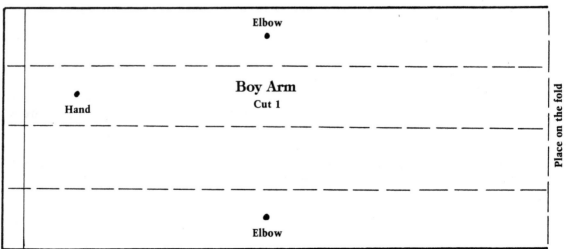

Elbow

**Boy Arm**
Cut 1

Hand

Elbow

**Place on the fold**

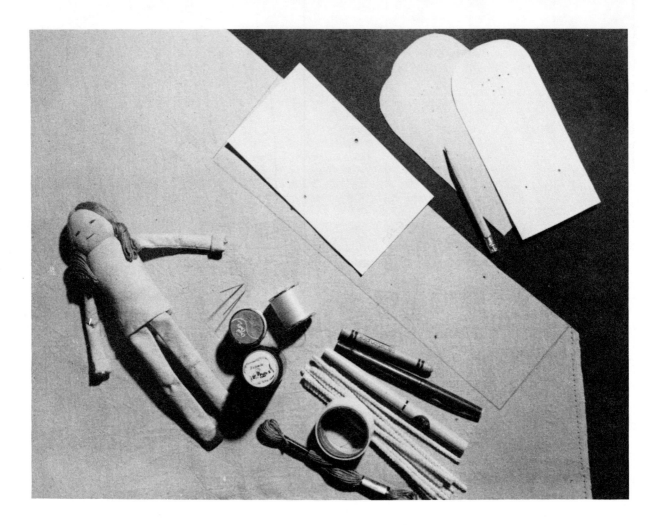

**Girl and Boy Doll Patterns,
pages 128 and 129**

*Cutting Out the Dressable Doll Pieces*
Place all pattern pieces on the fabric bias. Mark all dots. Note that you must flip the arm and leg patterns to get full length arm and leg sections.

STEP-BY-STEP: Head and Torso Piece
Follow the steps on page 95 for the Predressed Doll Head and Torso Piece, except for Step 4.

STEP-BY-STEP: Pipe Cleaner Arms
1. Bend a pipe cleaner smoothly around the end of a pencil to get an even curve (figure 6-24). This is the start of the arm joint.

6-24

2. Finish the 1¾" lower arm section by bending the middle part of the pipe cleaner around the pencil (figure 6-25) and twisting the end around the center (figure 6-26).

3. Form the upper arm section by bending another pipe cleaner around the pencil at one end and linking it through the loop of the lower arm section (figure 6-27). Then bend the middle part as in Step 2 and twist the end around the center.

4. Tape around the coiled pipe cleaner for added strength.

5. Fold and iron or pin to hold the arm fabric in place (figure 6-28).

6. Sew the lower arm joint loop to the arm fabric at the dots (figure 6-29). The tiny stitches will look like elbows.

7. Tuck in ¼" at each end (figure 6-29).

8. Fold, pin, and hand stitch along the long edge. Make the stitches as invisible as possible (figure 6-30).

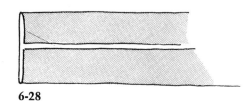

6-28

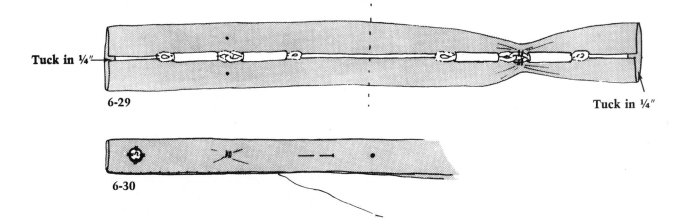

9. Sew on the hand snaps (figure 6-31). To make sure all the dolls' hands will match, always sew the snap with the hole on the right hand.

10. Fold the hand forward and sew it down with small hand stitches (figure 6-31).

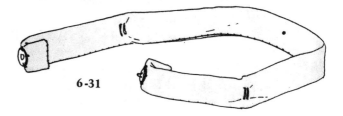

6-31

11. Matching center dots, sew the arm section to the back of the doll making sure the hands face front and the seam is at the bottom (figure 6-32).

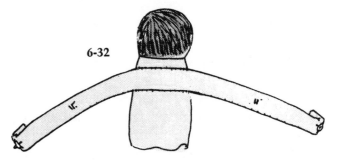

6-32

STEP-BY-STEP: Pipe Cleaner Legs

1. Bend the pipe cleaners for the legs in the same way you did for the arms but follow the dimensions in figure 6-33. Wrap an extra pipe cleaner around the longer leg section for added strength before wrapping it with tape.

6-33

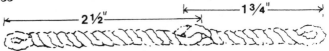

2½"    1¾"

2. Tuck in ½" at each end. Sew the lower joint loop to the fabric at the dots with tiny hand stitches (figure 6-34). The stitches will look like knees.

6-34

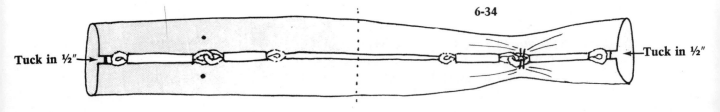

Tuck in ½"→    ←Tuck in ½"

3. Fold, pin, and hand stitch along the long edge (see figure 6-30). Make the stitches as invisible as possible.

4. Fold the leg section, having the seam face in (figure 6-35).

5. Tuck the leg section into the torso. Sew the sections together along the front and back of the legs (figure 6-36).

6. Paint on shoes (figure 6-37) with watered-down acrylic paint or felt-tip marker. The marker often bleeds, so test it first on a scrap.

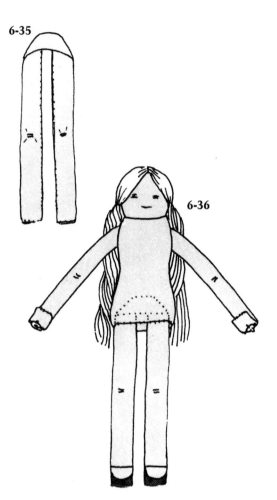

**6-35**

**6-36**

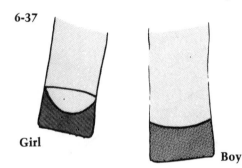

**6-37**

Girl

Boy

### Embroidered Face

When you embroider your dolls' faces you will give each one a distinct personality. No two will look exactly alike. Watch what effect the faces have upon your children. They will quickly note the different personalities of their dolls and invent life stories for each of them in their play.

Color Plate 16 is a close-up portrait of three of the dolls. Their eyes are simple straight stitches and French knots; their mouths are also straight stitched. Rosy cheeks can be easily added with crayons and freckles with felt-tip markers.

MATERIALS

Regular sewing thread, doubled. Use black, brown, blue, or whatever looks best with your doll's hair color (the hair is the next step). You can also use tiny seed beads.

- Make sure your starting and finishing knots end up on the back of the head where they will be covered with hair.

133

1. To outline the eyes, bring the needle up at the inner dot, then stitch over and under from dot to dot catching the upper line in the center (figures 6-38 a, b, c, d, e).

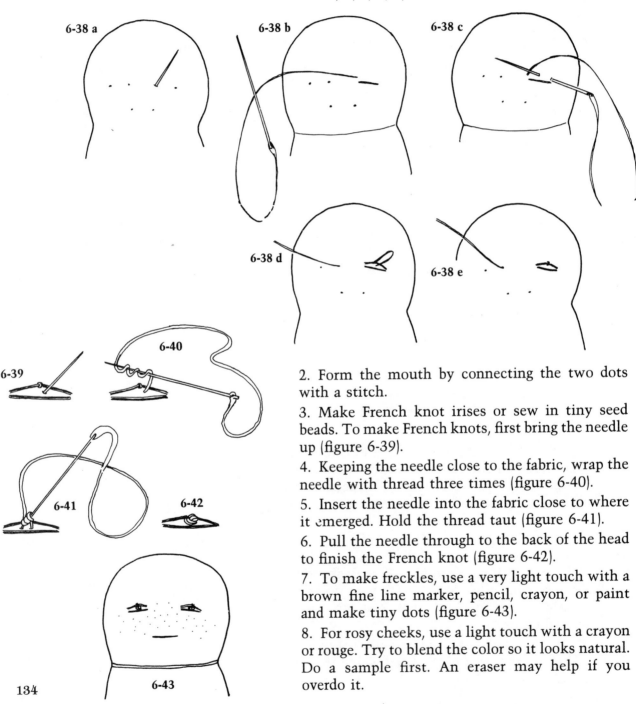

6-38 a

6-38 b

6-38 c

6-38 d

6-38 e

6-39

6-40

6-41

6-42

6-43

2. Form the mouth by connecting the two dots with a stitch.

3. Make French knot irises or sew in tiny seed beads. To make French knots, first bring the needle up (figure 6-39).

4. Keeping the needle close to the fabric, wrap the needle with thread three times (figure 6-40).

5. Insert the needle into the fabric close to where it emerged. Hold the thread taut (figure 6-41).

6. Pull the needle through to the back of the head to finish the French knot (figure 6-42).

7. To make freckles, use a very light touch with a brown fine line marker, pencil, crayon, or paint and make tiny dots (figure 6-43).

8. For rosy cheeks, use a light touch with a crayon or rouge. Try to blend the color so it looks natural. Do a sample first. An eraser may help if you overdo it.

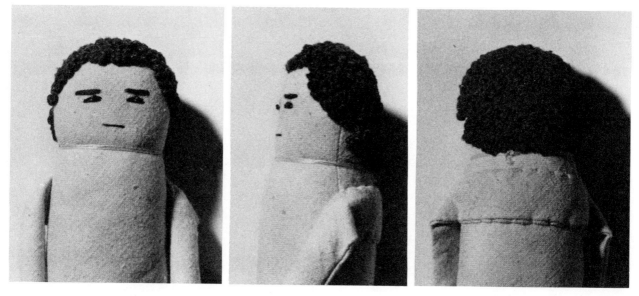

## Embroidered Hair

*French Knot Curly Hair (Color Plate 6)*

MATERIALS

One skein of six-strand embroidery floss in any hair color you like

STEP-BY-STEP

1. Draw the hairline lightly in pencil (figure 6-44).

2. Cut pieces of floss about one yard long. Double the thread in the needle. Bring the unknotted thread through the head. The stuffing will hold it in place (figure 6-44).

- Start the knots at the hairline and work around. If spaces are left, it is easy to go back and fill in.

3. Loop the thread once around the needle (figure 6-44).

4. Hold the thread taut. Take a tiny stitch and pull the needle through (figure 6-45). The finished knot and thread are in position for the next knot (figure 6-46).

5. Continue making knots close together until the head is covered (figure 6-47).

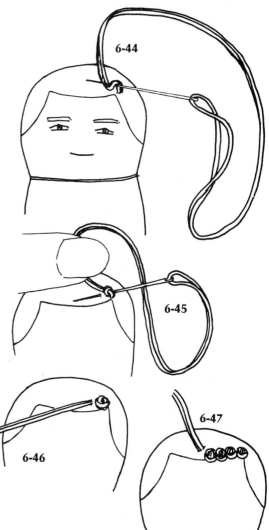

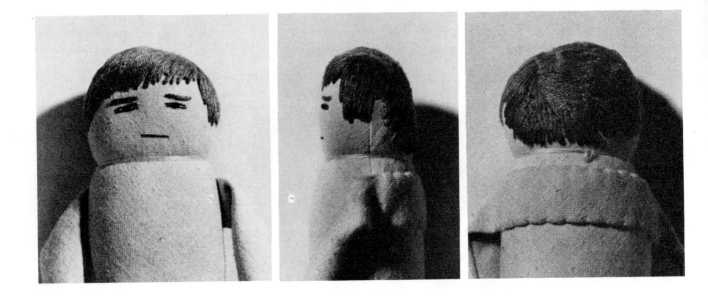

*Straight Hair for a Boy (Color Plate 12)*

**MATERIALS**

One skein of six-strand embroidery floss

**STEP-BY-STEP**

1. Draw a light pencil hairline and a part line (figure 6-48).

2. Use a single strand of the full thickness of floss. Don't knot the end of the thread. Bring the needle through the head so the stuffing holds the thread end in place.

3. Begin stitching at the part and work around and out (figure 6-49). Stitch over and under, making stitches about ½" long. Overlap layers about ¼". Stagger the stitches a bit so that the rows blend. If pulling the needle gets difficult, pull it carefully with a pair of small pliers.

**6-48**

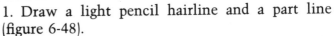
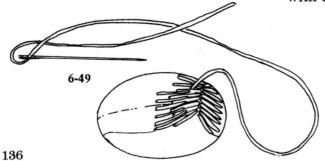

**6-49**

136

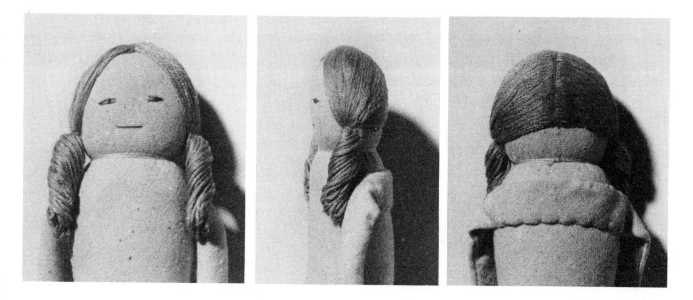

## Short Pigtails for a Girl (Color Plate 6)

MATERIALS

2½" X ½" strip of flesh colored fabric
One skein of six-strand embroidery floss
Sewing thread as close to the color of the floss as
possible

STEP-BY-STEP

1. Mark off a 1½" section on the fabric strip
(figure 6-50).

2. Remove the labels, but do not cut the floss.
Center and spread the floss evenly over the 1½"
section of fabric (figure 6-51).

**6-50**

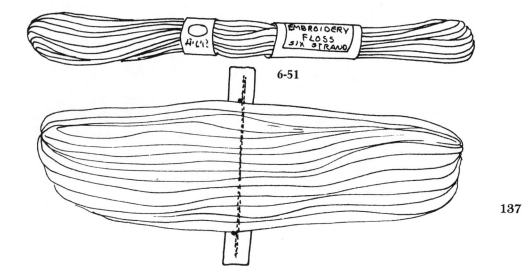

**6-51**

6-52

3. Sew the floss to the fabric first with a medium-length machine stitch, then go over it once or twice with a very small stitch. Or, sew it by hand with a small backstitch (figure 6-51). This stitching line forms the doll's part.

4. Place the hair on the doll's head. Tuck in the ends of the fabric strip, then attach it with hand backstitches along the part (figure 6-52). Then smooth the hair in place and sew around the pigtails by hand, sewing them to the doll's head (figure 6-52). Wet the pigtails and twist them tightly; when they dry they will have a "natural" curl.

*Long Hair for a Girl (Color Plate 19)*

MATERIALS

Three skeins of six-strand embroidery floss
2½" X ½" fabric strip

- Hair will look very natural if you use two skeins of one color and one skein of a slightly different shade. For brown hair: two skeins dark colonial brown and one skein dark brown. For blond hair: two skeins yellow and one skein ecru.

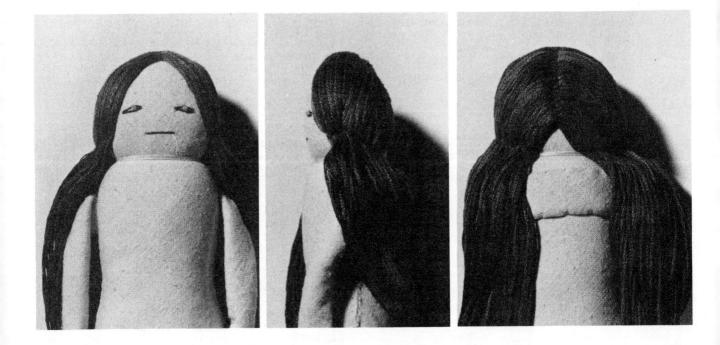

1. Mark off a 1¾″ section on the fabric strip (figure 6-53).

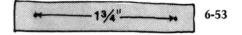

**6-53**

2. Cut the skeins on one end only (figure 6-54) and open them out.

**6-54**

3. Spread two skeins over the 1¾″ section of fabric; distribute the third slightly different color skein on top of them (figure 6-55).

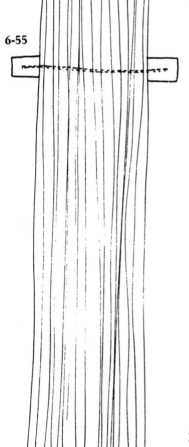

**6-55**

**6-56**

139

**6-57**

4. Sew the floss to the fabric first with a medium-length machine stitch, then go over it once or twice with a very small stitch (figure 6-55). You can also sew by hand with a small backstitch. This stitching line is the doll's part.

5. Place the hair on the doll's head. Tuck in the ends of the fabric strip and sew it by hand, backstitching along the part and along the side (figure 6-56). You may have to go back and forth several times to catch all the floss in the stitching.

*Fancy Hairdos (Color Plate 16)*

To give your dolls fancy hairdos, first follow Steps 1 to 5 for Long Hair for a Girl, page 138.

- To make braids, braid the hair and tie at the bottom with thread (figure 6-58).
- Twist the braids toward the back and sew or pin in position (figure 6-57).
- For wavy hair, wet the braids; let them dry, then unbraid them (figure 6-59).

**6-58**

**6-59**

- Twist the hair tightly until it winds back on itself (figure 6-60). The twists will stay in place temporarily on their own; you can also sew or pin them in place (figure 6-61).
- Place pretty party favor flowers in their hair for an extra-special look.

6-60

6-61

## DRESSABLE BABY DOLL

STEP-BY-STEP

1. Make the head and torso as for the Predressed Baby Doll, page 126, but do not sew the bottom closed in Step 4.

2. Fold and sew the arms and legs (figure 6-62) as for the big dolls but leave out the pipe cleaners and the snaps (see page 131). Sew the arm section to the back.

**Baby Doll Patterns, page 143**

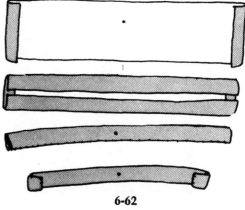

6-62

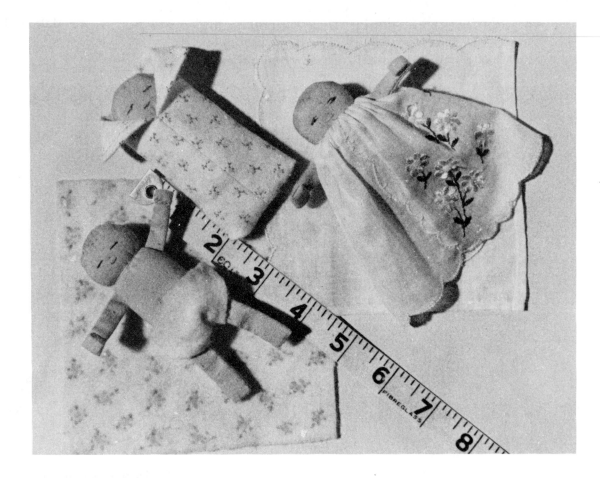

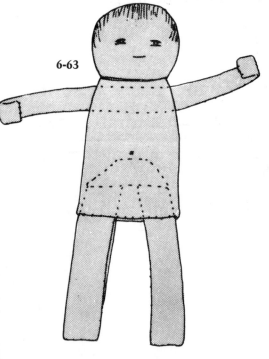

6-63

3. Sew and tuck in the legs as for the big dolls (figure 6-63).

4. Make a small stitch for a belly button (figure 6-63).

### Diaper

Cut the diaper from felt or polyester fleece interlining (figure 6-64). Sew on two snaps.

### Bunting for the Dressable Baby

To make a removable bunting for the Dressable Baby Doll, cut the fabric to the same width as the predressed baby bunting, page 126, but increase the length to 5¼". Then follow the instructions.

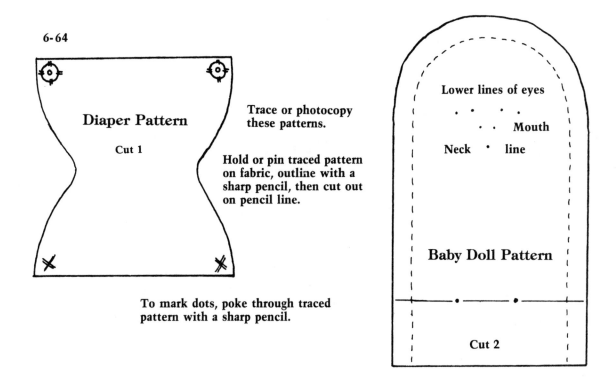

**Diaper Pattern**

Cut 1

Trace or photocopy
these patterns.

Hold or pin traced pattern
on fabric, outline with a
sharp pencil, then cut out
on pencil line.

To mark dots, poke through traced
pattern with a sharp pencil.

Lower lines of eyes

Mouth

Neck · line

**Baby Doll Pattern**

Cut 2

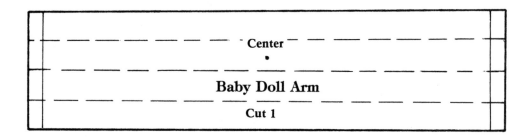

Center

**Baby Doll Arm**

Cut 1

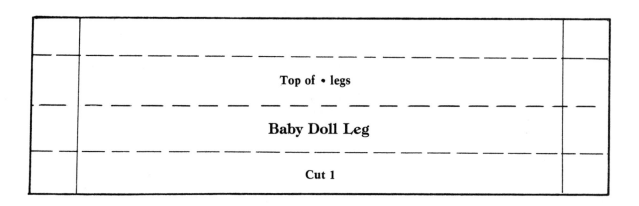

Top of · legs

**Baby Doll Leg**

Cut 1

# 7
# Casual Clothing

Your dolls' wardrobe can consist of the latest in tops and slacks, knit dresses and sweaters, and even bathing suits! Each item is made from such a small piece of fabric that it's likely you can fashion an entire stylish wardrobe just from fabric scraps you have on hand.

Included in the clothing chapters are many Learn-to-Sew projects to help little ones practice some basic techniques—tracing, cutting on the lines, sewing a seam. The step-by-step instructions for the Learn-to-Sew projects are more detailed so that a child can follow them without too much assistance and can achieve the pleasure of accomplishment.

Also included is an edge-finishing technique which makes sewing the clothes especially easy for children and quick for you. The technique provides durable, non-ravelling edges with no sewing. In Step 1 of all projects that call for this technique you will find a quick reference to the white glue technique page. Clothing made with this technique should not be washed or dry cleaned.

Most of the clothing is for the Dressable Dolls but the Predressed Dolls can wear some of the Learn-to-Sew outfits.

# WHITE GLUE TECHNIQUE FOR FINISHING EDGES

### STEP-BY-STEP

1. Pencil around the pattern outline onto the fabric.

2. Place waxed paper under the fabric. Go over the pencil line with white glue (figure 7-1). Blend the glue into the fabric with your finger, spreading it into a trail about ¼" wide.

3. When the glue is thoroughly dry, cut out the fabric along the pencil lines.

## A BASIC WARDROBE

### Teddy

### MATERIALS

You can make a pretty teddy from the lace top of an infant's anklet (size 5½ to 6½). You could also use any lightweight jersey fabric or a piece of an old T-shirt.

### STEP-BY-STEP

1. Cut off the 3" length (figure 7-2).

2. Sew close to the cut edge with tiny machine stitches to prevent running (figure 7-3).

3. Turn a hem to the outside and sew by hand at the center top and bottom (figure 7-4).

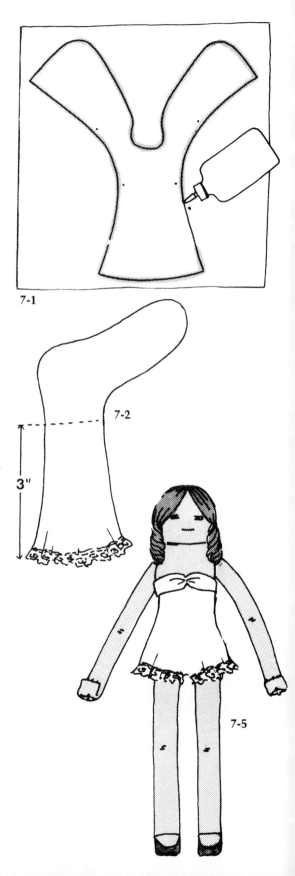

7-1

7-2

3"

7-5

7-3

7-4

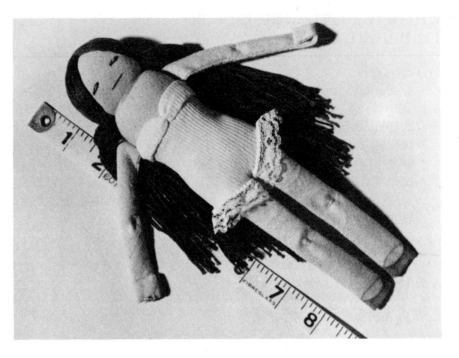

## Shorts

**MATERIALS**

Make a pair of shorts from an infant's stretch sock, bits of an old T-shirt, or any lightweight jersey material.

**STEP-BY-STEP**

1. Cut off the 1⅝" length (figure 7-7).

2. Sew close to the cut edge with tiny machine stitches to prevent running (figure 7-8).

3. Hand stitch the leg hems and at center bottom (figure 7-9).

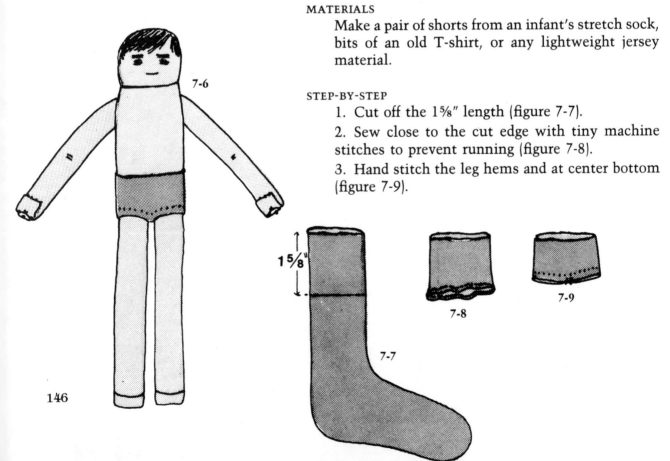

7-6

1 ⅝"

7-7

7-8

7-9

146

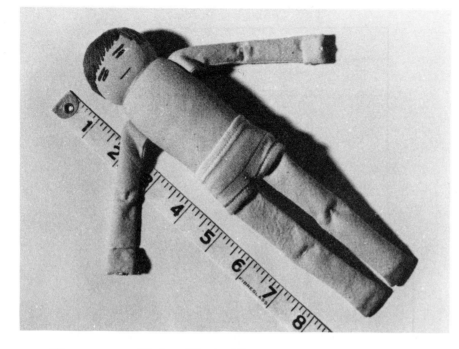

## Sleepwear (Color Plate 8)

Follow the instructions for the Fairy Tale Gown, page 187, to make a pretty nightgown, but use flannel material. To make a pair of pajamas, make one of the shirts on page 151 or 153 and the pants below out of lightweight fabric.

## Pants for a Boy or Girl Doll (Color Plate 6)

Pants Pattern, page 148

MATERIALS

Light- to medium-weight fabrics such as cotton broadcloth or felt make great-looking slacks. Blue chambray shirt material is a good stand-in for denim. Stiff, heavy fabrics (like real denim) will not work well. You'll need one snap.

● Note the different cutting lines for felt and for other fabrics on the pattern. Felt needs only a single turned hem.

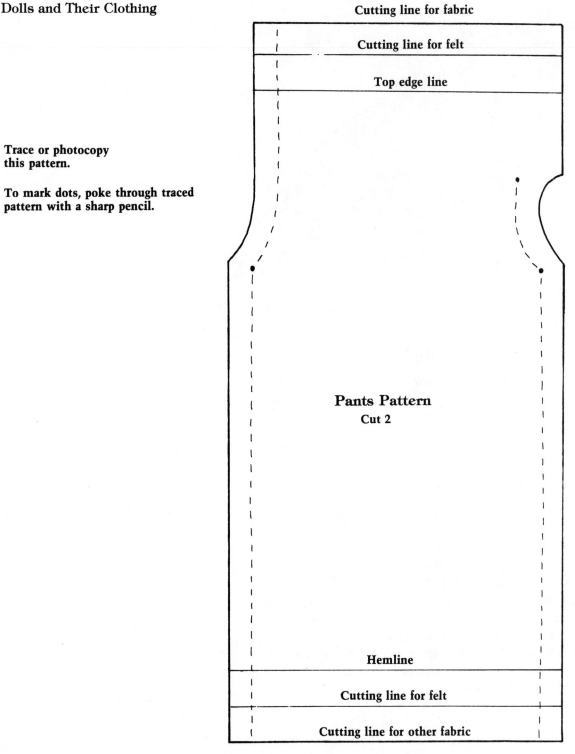

Trace or photocopy
this pattern.

To mark dots, poke through traced
pattern with a sharp pencil.

Cutting line for fabric

Cutting line for felt

Top edge line

**Pants Pattern**
**Cut 2**

Hemline

Cutting line for felt

Cutting line for other fabric

1. Turn the top seam allowance down toward the right side of the fabric to form the waistband and sew (figure 7-10).

2. Finish the pants bottoms by turning the fabric to the right side for cuffs and to the wrong side for plain bottoms. Sew (figure 7-10).

3. Sew the front and back seams right sides together (figure 7-11).

4. Sew the leg seams just to the center seams but not over them; backstitch (figure 7-12).

5. Sew on the snap to fit at the waist (figure 7-13).

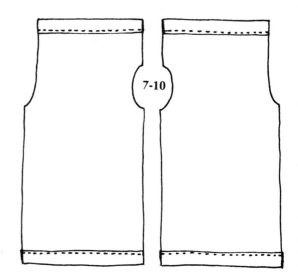

7-10

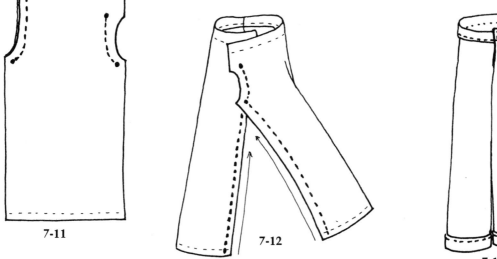

7-11

7-12

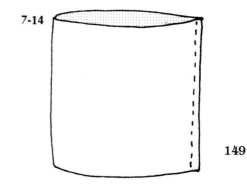

7-13

## Skirt

### Skirt Pattern, page 150

MATERIALS

Light- to medium-weight fabric
6″ of elastic cord

STEP-BY-STEP

1. Cut out the skirt. The pattern is for a just below the knee length, but you can cut the skirt to whatever length you like.

2. With right sides together, sew the seam (figure 7-14).

7-14

149

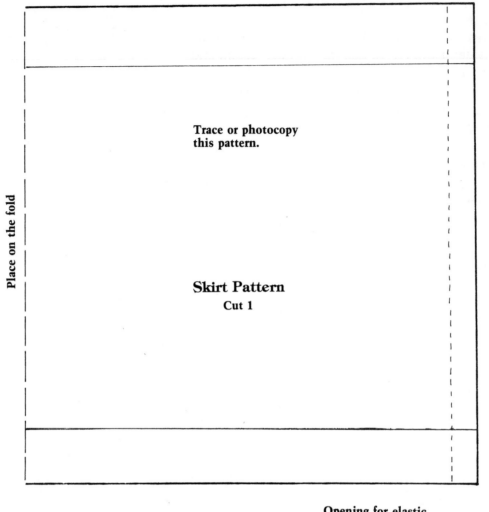

**Place on the fold**

Trace or photocopy
this pattern.

**Skirt Pattern**
Cut 1

**Opening for elastic**

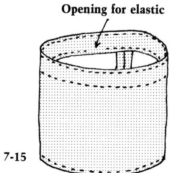

7-15

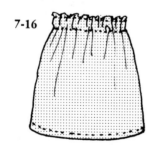

7-16

3. Hem the bottom (figure 7-15). Sew a ⅜″ casing at the top leaving a ¼″ opening for the elastic (figure 7-15).

4. Insert the elastic cord and tie the skirt on the doll (figure 7-16).

# Collarless Shirt/Blouse

MATERIALS
Light- to medium-weight fabric
Two snaps

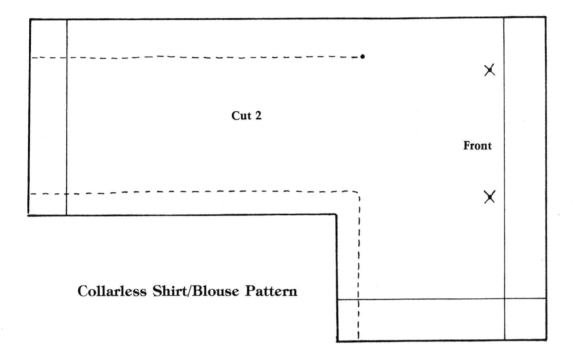

**Cut 2**

Front

**Collarless Shirt/Blouse Pattern**

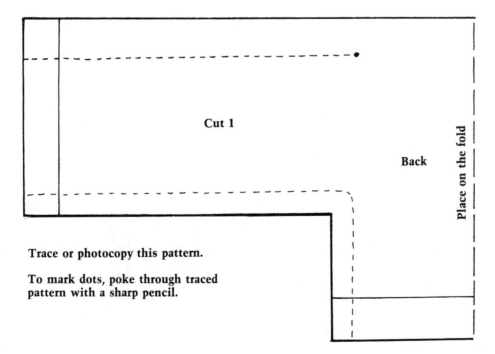

**Cut 1**

Back

Place on the fold

Trace or photocopy this pattern.

To mark dots, poke through traced
pattern with a sharp pencil.

STEP-BY-STEP

1. Sew the shoulder seams right sides together to the dots (figure 7-17).

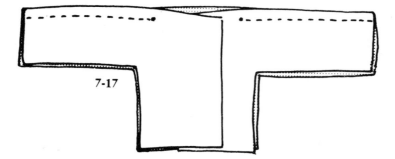

7-17

2. Turn down the seam allowances at the shoulders and neck and stitch (figure 7-18).

7-18

3. Sew the side seams, the bottom hem, then the front edges and sleeve hems by hand. Clip (figure 7-19).

7-19

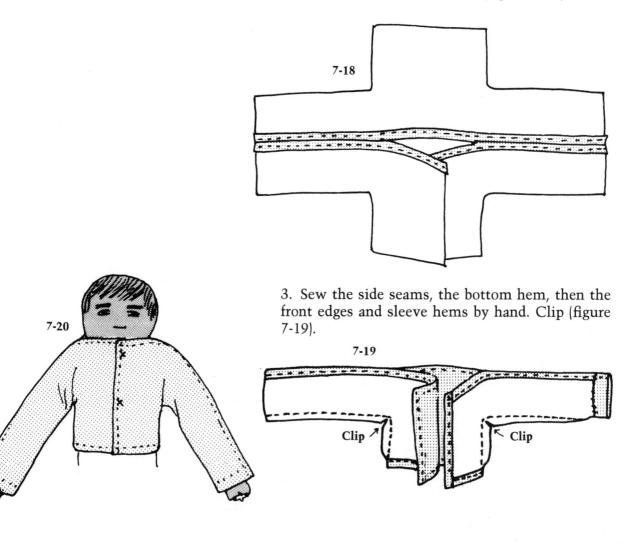

7-20

Clip

Clip

4. Sew on the snaps (figure 7-20). The shirt/blouse can be worn with the opening in the back or the front.

## Shirt with a Collar (Color Plate 11)

**Shirt with a Collar Pattern,
page 154**

MATERIALS
Light- to medium-weight fabric
Two snaps

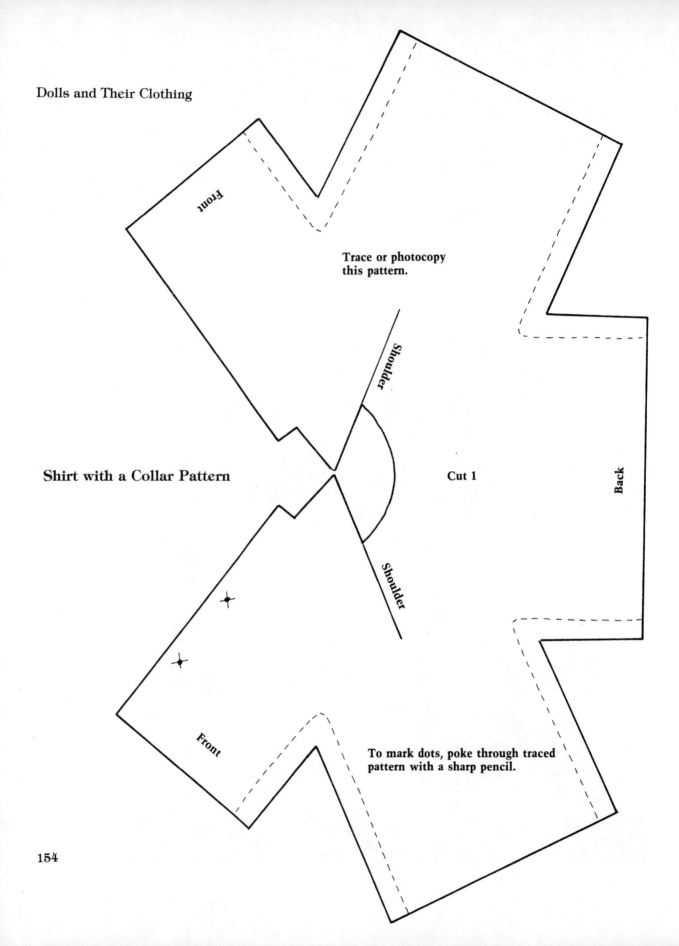

Front

Trace or photocopy
this pattern.

Shoulder

**Shirt with a Collar Pattern**

Cut 1

Back

Shoulder

Front

To mark dots, poke through traced
pattern with a sharp pencil.

1. Cut out the fabric using the white glue technique, page 145.

2. With fabric right sides together, sew ¼″ side and sleeve seams. Clip at the underarm (figure 7-21).

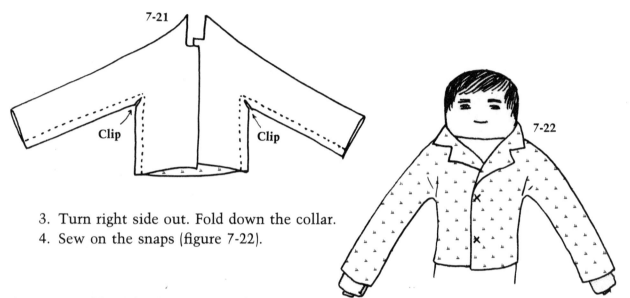

7-21

Clip        Clip

7-22

3. Turn right side out. Fold down the collar.

4. Sew on the snaps (figure 7-22).

## SOCK CLOTHES (Color Plate 6)

These wonderfully easy-to-make sock dresses and hats look like expensive knit outfits.

MATERIALS

Children's socks, sizes 5 to 9, or adults' stretch socks (see figures 7-23 and 7-25)

### Sundress and Hat

STEP-BY-STEP

1. Cut the sock into sections (figure 7-23).

2. For the hat, simply roll up a brim—there's no sewing involved!

3. To make the dress, turn down the sock cuff partway for the bodice (figure 7-24). To prevent running, sew around the bottom raw edge with a small machine stitch. Then roll or turn a bottom hem (figure 7-24).

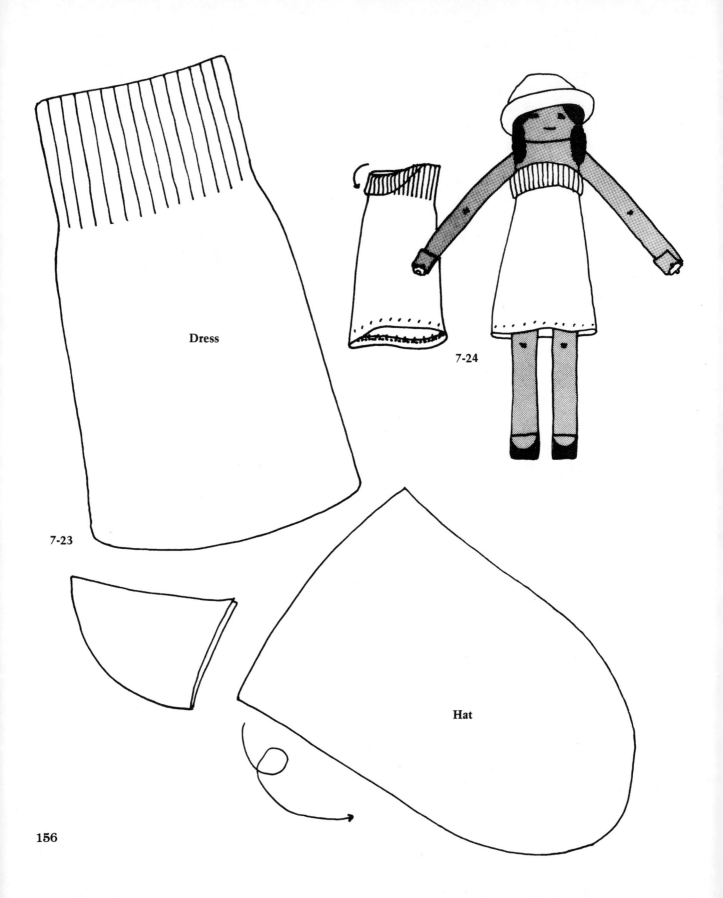

Dress

7-24

7-23

Hat

## Sweater

STEP-BY-STEP

1. Cut the sock into sections (figure 7-25). Slit the sock where indicated for the armholes. The length of the slit may vary according to the size sock you're using. Cut the slits to fit your sleeves.

2. Sew around all cut edges with a small machine stitch to prevent runs (figure 7-26).

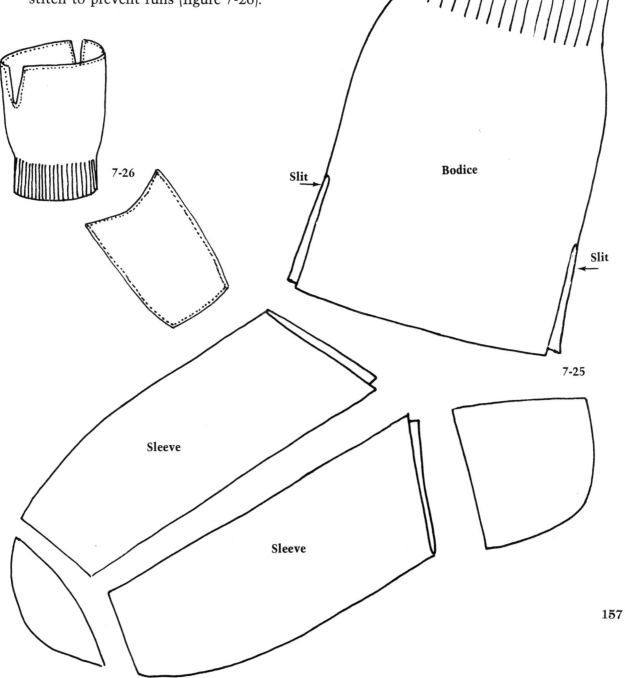

7-26

Slit

Bodice

Slit

7-25

Sleeve

Sleeve

157

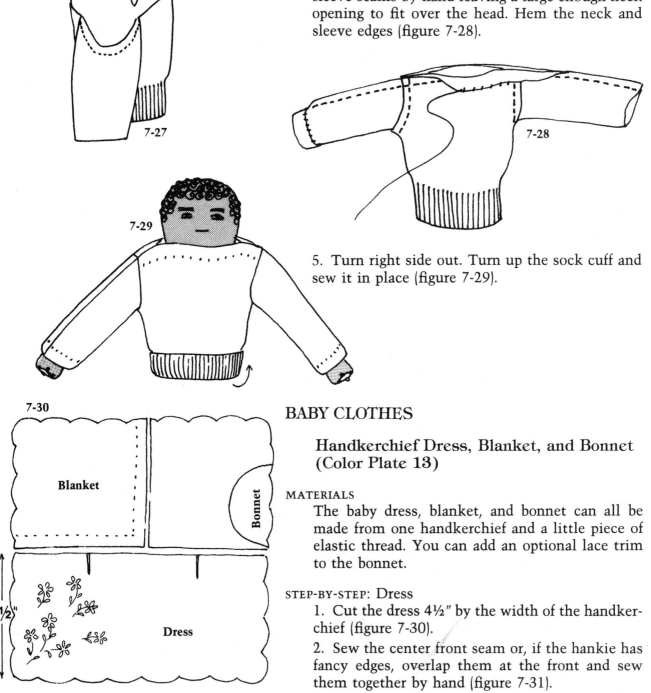

7-27

7-28

7-29

7-30

Blanket

Bonnet

Dress

4½"

3. Set in the sleeve making sure right sides of the sleeve and bodice are together (figure 7-27). *The sleeve seam will be on top.*

4. With wrong side out, sew the shoulder and sleeve seams by hand leaving a large enough neck opening to fit over the head. Hem the neck and sleeve edges (figure 7-28).

5. Turn right side out. Turn up the sock cuff and sew it in place (figure 7-29).

## BABY CLOTHES

### Handkerchief Dress, Blanket, and Bonnet (Color Plate 13)

MATERIALS

The baby dress, blanket, and bonnet can all be made from one handkerchief and a little piece of elastic thread. You can add an optional lace trim to the bonnet.

STEP-BY-STEP: Dress

1. Cut the dress 4½" by the width of the handkerchief (figure 7-30).

2. Sew the center front seam or, if the hankie has fancy edges, overlap them at the front and sew them together by hand (figure 7-31).

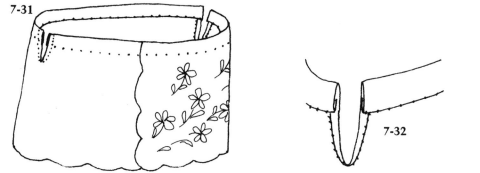

7-31

7-32

7-33

3. Cut 1½" slits at the sides for armholes (figure 7-31). Hem around the armholes by hand (figure 7-32). Then make a ⅜" casing along the top edge (figure 7-31). Turn right side out.

4. Insert the elastic thread and tie it together (figure 7-33).

STEP-BY-STEP: Bonnet

1. Turn under a ¼" hem around the curved edge. Straight stitch and gather (figure 7-34).

2. You can add lace to finished bonnet (figure 7-35).

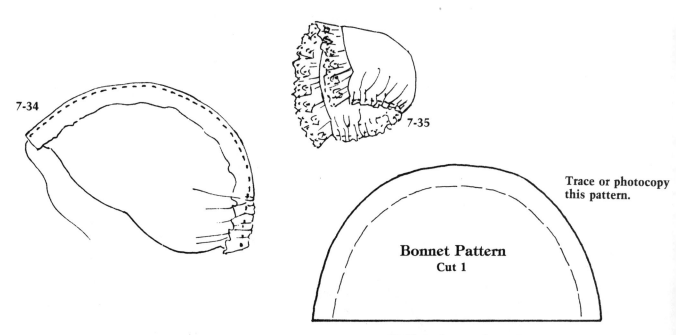

7-34

7-35

Trace or photocopy this pattern.

**Bonnet Pattern**
Cut 1

Hold or pin traced pattern on fabric, outline with a sharp pencil, then cut out on pencil line.

STEP-BY-STEP: Blanket

Simply hem the two raw edges (figure 7-30).

# Wraparound Playsuit

**MATERIALS**

You can use cotton calicos or flannels for this playsuit. Or you can draw a simple design with a felt-tip marker on white felt or polyester fleece interlining.

**STEP-BY-STEP**

1. Use the white glue technique, page 145, to trace, glue, and cut out the fabric.

● If you use felt or fleece there is no need to glue the edges. Simply cut.

7-36

7-37

**Wraparound Playsuit Pattern**

**Cut 1**

2. Place the playsuit right side down on a surface. Place the doll over the suit (figure 7-36). Bring the top over the shoulders and the bottom between the legs (figure 7-37). Tie the tabs in the back or sew on snaps if you like (figure 7-38).

## Wrap-Up Blanket

MATERIALS

5″ square of white felt, polyester fleece interlining, or woven fabric

STEP-BY-STEP

1. Draw a simple design in felt-tip marker or a 5″ square of felt or polyester fleece interlining. These fabrics do not need hemming.

2. Fringe or hem if you use woven fabric.

3. Sew on a snap (figure 7-39) and wrap up the baby (figure 7-40).

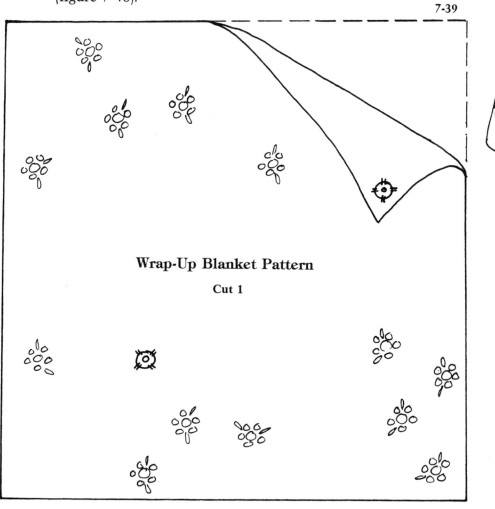

7-38

7-40

7-39

**Wrap-Up Blanket Pattern**

**Cut 1**

**Trace or photocopy this pattern.**

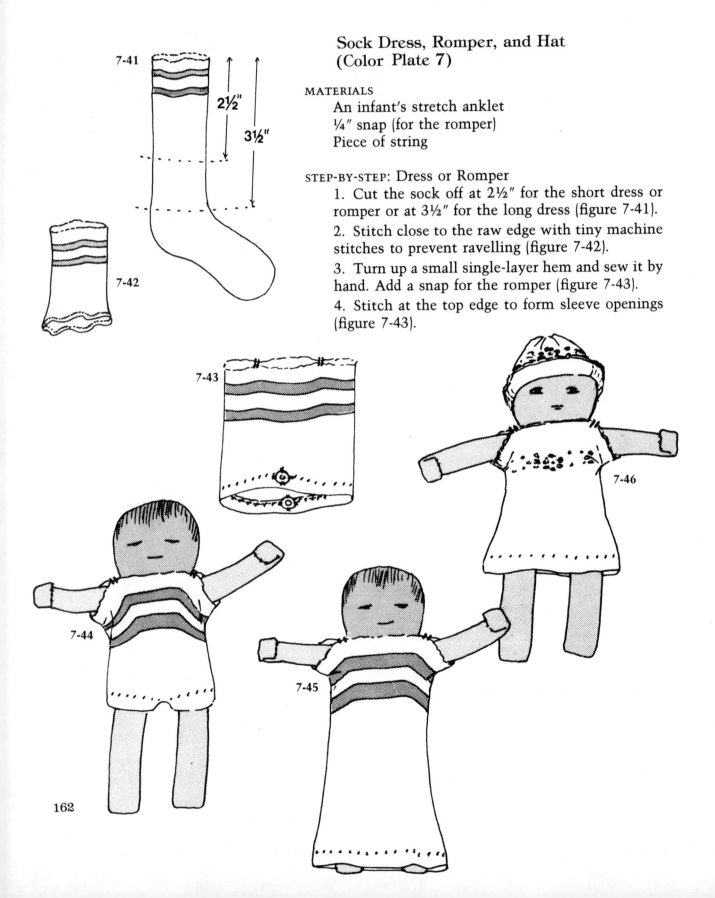

**Sock Dress, Romper, and Hat
(Color Plate 7)**

MATERIALS
An infant's stretch anklet
¼" snap (for the romper)
Piece of string

STEP-BY-STEP: Dress or Romper

1. Cut the sock off at 2½" for the short dress or romper or at 3½" for the long dress (figure 7-41).

2. Stitch close to the raw edge with tiny machine stitches to prevent ravelling (figure 7-42).

3. Turn up a small single-layer hem and sew it by hand. Add a snap for the romper (figure 7-43).

4. Stitch at the top edge to form sleeve openings (figure 7-43).

7-41

2½"

3½"

7-42

7-43

7-44

7-45

7-46

STEP-BY-STEP: Hat

1. Cut out the hat piece (figure 7-47).
2. With wrong sides together, sew the seam (figure 7-48).
3. Gather in the top by tying with a piece of string (figure 7-49). Turn.
4. Turn up a brim (figure 7-50).

7-48

7-49

7-50

7-47

2¼"

1¼"

## LEARN-TO-SEW PROJECTS FOR CHILDREN

**Felt Vest Pattern, page 164**

**The dolls are warm and comfortable in their learn-to-sew felt vests and hats.**

Front

Front

Trace onto butcher paper to make a
sturdy pattern children can keep.

To mark dots, poke through traced
pattern with a sharp pencil.

Vest back

**Felt Vest Pattern**
Cut 1

Front

ఇ➤ Learn-to-Sew: Felt Vest (Color Plate 3)

Both the predressed and the dressable dolls can
wear this easy-to-make felt vest. The dolls in the picture on page 163 are wearing this vest.

1. Cut out the fabric using the pattern. Transfer the dots by poking through the pattern with a sharp pencil.

2. Fold the vest wrong side out at the shoulders. Pin it and then sew to the dots (figure 7-51).

### ᔰ Learn-to-Sew: Bolero Vest

Both predressed and dressable dolls can wear this bolero vest.

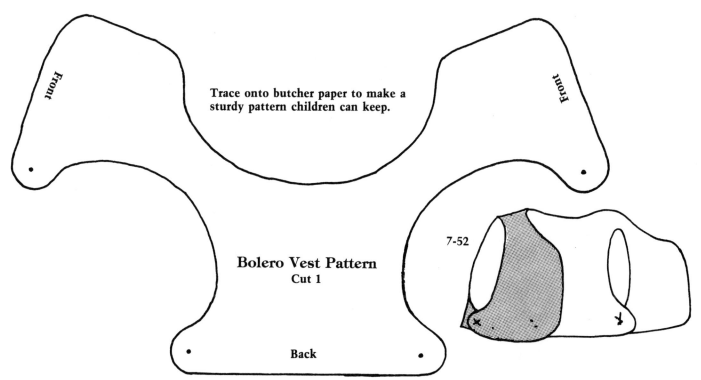

7-51

Trace onto butcher paper to make a sturdy pattern children can keep.

**Front** **Front**

**Bolero Vest Pattern**
Cut 1

**Back**

7-52

MATERIALS

You can make this vest from felt or from other fabric using the white glue technique on page 145 or from lightweight suede or leather.

STEP-BY-STEP

1. Pin the pattern on the felt. Mark the dots and either cut right around the pattern or outline the pattern with pencil, then cut out on the pencil line.

2. Sew the sides together (figure 7-52).

3. If you like, you can glue or sew on sequins or small beads for a very fancy bolero vest.

7-53

## ॐ Learn-to-Sew: Apron (Color Plate 5)

**MATERIALS**

3″ square piece of fabric
14″ piece of ⅝″ bias tape

**STEP-BY-STEP**

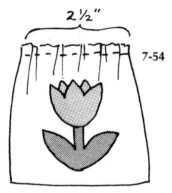

1. Either finish the sides and bottom edges of the fabric with the white glue technique, page 145, before cutting out the 3″ square, or cut it out and fringe the edges.

- Gingham makes fringing especially easy.
- You can draw a crayon design onto plain fabric (see page 46 for how to set the color).

2. Gather the top edge to 2½″ (figure 7-54).

3. Place the upper fold of the bias tape over the apron, right sides together (figure 7-55). Sew them together.

4. Fold the tape over to the back of the apron. Sew it with small hand stitches (figure 7-56).

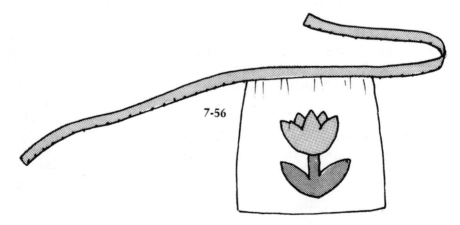

# ❧ Learn-to-Sew: Cap (Color Plate 5)

STEP-BY-STEP

1. Pencil around the cap pattern onto the fabric.

2. Use the white glue technique, page 145, to finish the edges. Then cut out the circle.

3. With short running stitches, gather the inside circle (figure 7-57).

4. Fit the cap to the doll's head.

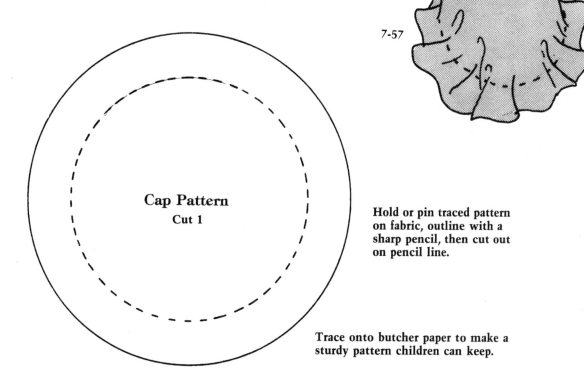

7-57

**Cap Pattern**
Cut 1

Hold or pin traced pattern on fabric, outline with a sharp pencil, then cut out on pencil line.

Trace onto butcher paper to make a sturdy pattern children can keep.

# ❧ Learn-to-Sew: Wrap Dress or Jumper

With unfinished edges this dress is quick and easy for children to make. For a more durable dress you can finish the edges with the white glue technique on page 145 before you cut out the dress.

**Wrap Dress or Jumper Pattern, page 168**

MATERIALS

12″ square fabric piece

12″ of ¼″ or ½″ wide ribbon, bias tape, rickrack, or braid (optional, for belt)

7″ of narrow lace (optional)

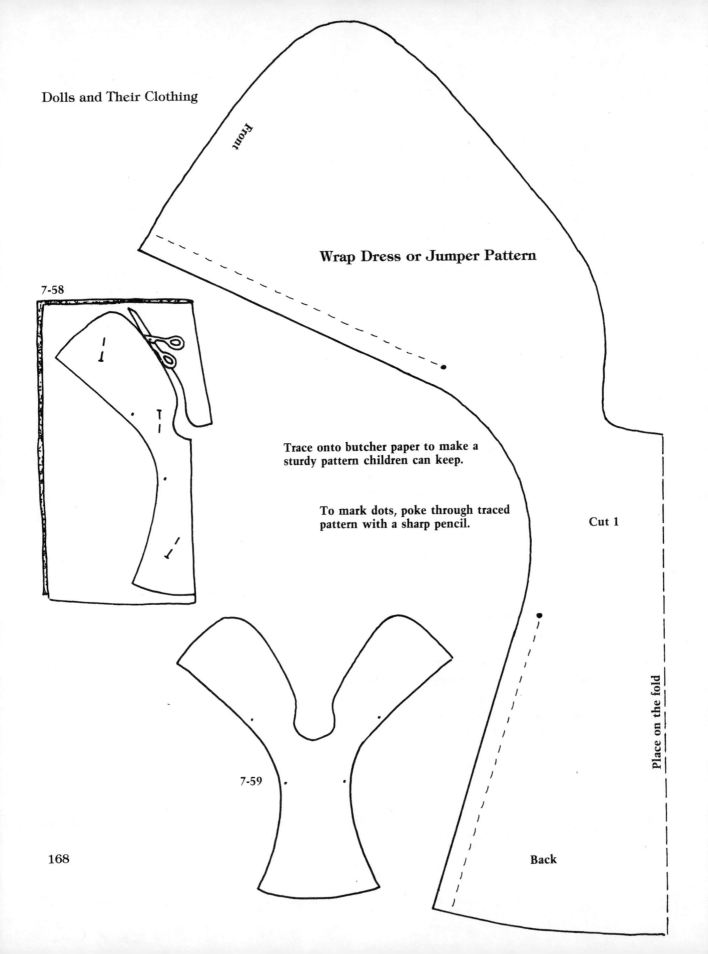

Dolls and Their Clothing

Front

Wrap Dress or Jumper Pattern

7-58

Trace onto butcher paper to make a
sturdy pattern children can keep.

To mark dots, poke through traced
pattern with a sharp pencil.

Cut 1

Place on the fold

7-59

168

Back

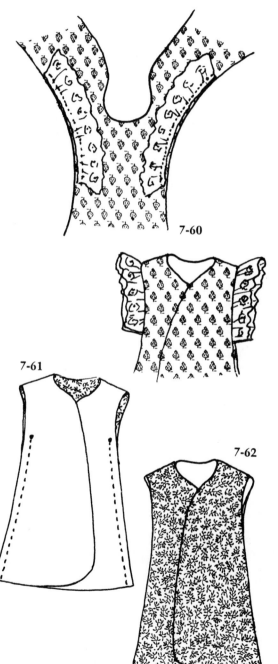

7-60

7-61

7-62

STEP-BY-STEP

1. Fold the fabric in half, right sides together. Place the pattern on the fold and pin (figure 7-58). Cut out the fabric.

2. Open out the fabric. Pierce through the pattern with a pencil onto the wrong side of the fabric to mark the dots (figure 7-59).

3. If you like, you can add trim between the two dots at the jumper shoulders by sewing the trim to the right or wrong side of the fabric, whatever looks best (figure 7-60).

4. Sew the side seams wrong side out (figure 7-61).

5. Turn the dress right side out (figure 7-62).

6. If you're not using ribbon, cut out a ¼″ wide strip of self-fabric, 12″ long, for a sash.

7. The dress and sash can be worn either way around.

# ACCESSORIES

## Tote Bag (Color Plate 9)

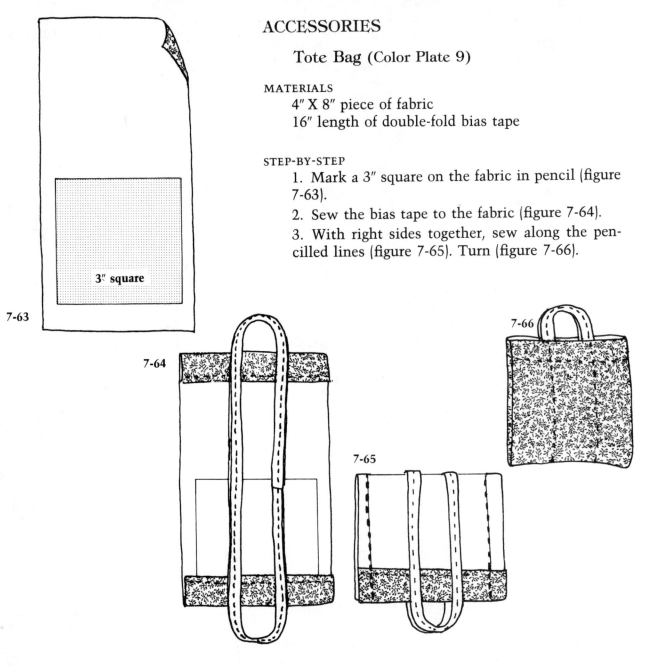

**MATERIALS**
4″ X 8″ piece of fabric
16″ length of double-fold bias tape

**STEP-BY-STEP**
1. Mark a 3″ square on the fabric in pencil (figure 7-63).
2. Sew the bias tape to the fabric (figure 7-64).
3. With right sides together, sew along the pencilled lines (figure 7-65). Turn (figure 7-66).

7-63

3″ square

7-64

7-65

7-66

## Briefcase

By changing the dimensions of the Tote Bag slightly you can make a briefcase using lightweight suede, leather, or felt. Follow the instructions for the Tote Bag but sew the briefcase right side out. The briefcase piece measures 3″ by 5″ before folding. The briefcase is pictured on page 172.

## Knitting (Color Plate 22)

MATERIALS
Knitted sock
Two plastic toothpicks or wooden toothpicks
with points filed down
White glue

STEP-BY-STEP
1. Cut out a 3″ square from the sock (figure 7-67).

2. Sew around the three raw edges with a small stitch to prevent ravelling.

3. Slip the stitch loops along the top of the sock piece onto the toothpicks and glue them in the position you like (figure 7-68).

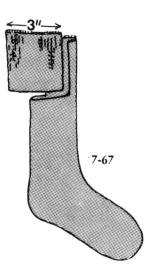

7-67

## Books (Color Plate 23)

Cut the book cover from colored construction paper. Use figure 7-69 as a pattern. Cut the pages a little bit smaller from white paper and staple or sew them to the cover in the center. Fold the book closed (figure 7-70).

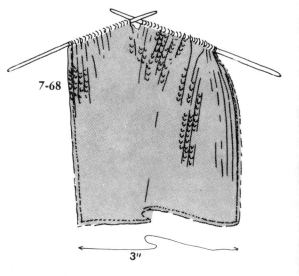

7-68

7-69

7-70

## Newspaper (Color Plate 14)

Cut pages from newspapers, the width of two narrow columns. Fold them in half and staple or sew them together along the fold (figure 7-71).

## Balls (Color Plate 13)

Balls for the baby dolls and pets to play with can be cut from ball fringe.

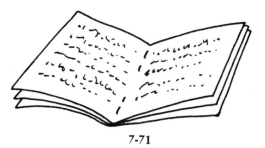

7-71

# 8

# Dress-Up and Fairy Tale Clothing

When the time comes for the dolls to go out on the town or when your child's imagination is inspired, this is the chapter to turn to. For here are included some fancy and fanciful clothes that are sure to please your youngster. There's a suit for the boy doll and evening gowns for the girl, wedding outfits, special attire for a prince and princess, even a shirt to be worn by an intergalactic traveller!

## ON THE TOWN

### Boy's Suit (Color Plate 13)

Jacket Pattern, page 174
Pants Pattern, page 148

The suit jacket and pants are made of felt. The jacket is especially easy to make from the all-in-one-piece pattern. If you like, you can make a sports jacket and complementary pants instead of a suit. You can use any appropriate fabric for the pants but the jacket is best in felt.

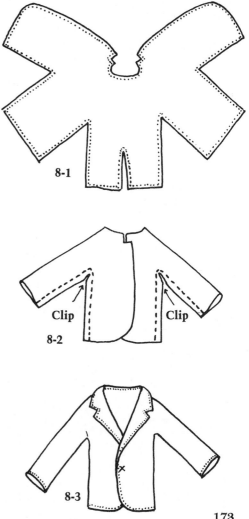

*Jacket*

MATERIALS
9" X 12" piece of felt
One snap

STEP-BY-STEP

1. With a small machine stitch or by hand, sew close to the edge all around the jacket (figure 8-1). This will protect the felt and give the garment a realistic topstitched look.

2. With right sides together, sew the ¼" side/sleeve seams. Clip (figure 8-2). Turn.

3. Add a snap to the front (figure 8-3).

*Pants*

MATERIALS
Felt to match the jacket or any light- to medium-weight fabric.
● Note the different cutting lines for felt and for other fabrics on the pattern. Felt needs only a single turned hem.
One snap

173

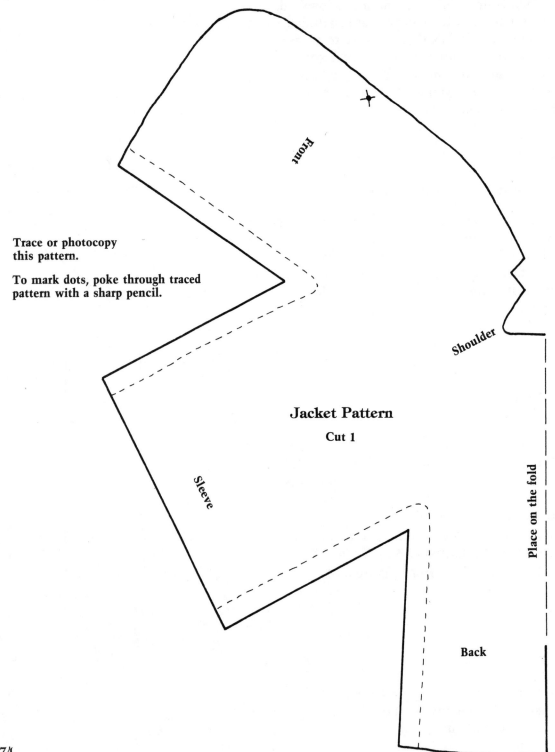

Trace or photocopy
this pattern.

To mark dots, poke through traced
pattern with a sharp pencil.

Front

Shoulder

Jacket Pattern

Cut 1

Sleeve

Place on the fold

Back

1. Turn the top seam allowance down toward the right side of the fabric to form the waistband and sew (figure 8-4).

2. Finish the pants bottoms by turning the fabric to the right side for cuffs and to the wrong side for plain bottoms. Sew (figure 8-4).

3. Sew the front and back seams right sides together (figure 8-5).

4. Sew the leg seams just to the center seams but not over them; backstitch (figure 8-6).

5. Turn right side out and sew a snap at the waist (figure 8-7).

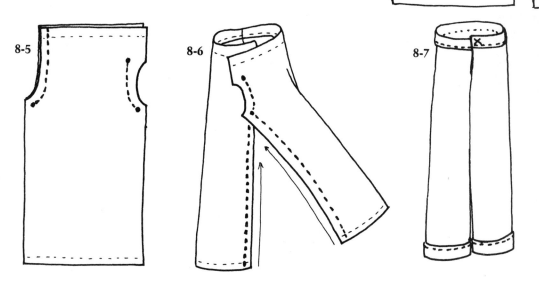

8-4

8-5

8-6

8-7

## Dress Shirt

**Dress Shirt Pattern, page 176**

Since it would be difficult to put a suit jacket on over shirt sleeves, the dress shirt consists only of a biblike front section. It ties around the neck.

### MATERIALS

Medium-weight non-woven interfacing or other medium-weight fabric

### STEP-BY-STEP

1. If you are using regular fabric, finish the edges with white glue (see page 145 for technique). If you use interfacing, just cut out the fabric.

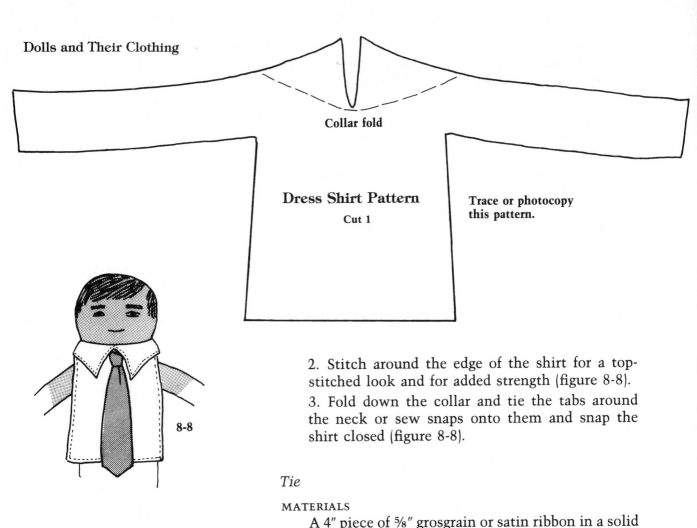

**Collar fold**

**Dress Shirt Pattern**
Cut 1

**Trace or photocopy this pattern.**

2. Stitch around the edge of the shirt for a top-stitched look and for added strength (figure 8-8).

3. Fold down the collar and tie the tabs around the neck or sew snaps onto them and snap the shirt closed (figure 8-8).

*Tie*

MATERIALS

A 4″ piece of ⅝″ grosgrain or satin ribbon in a solid color or a print is enough for one tie. For a beautiful striped tie, draw diagonal stripes on white satin ribbon with felt-tip markers.

STEP-BY-STEP

1. Fold the end of the ribbon lengthwise, right side out (figure 8-9) and tie an overhand knot at the top (figure 8-10).

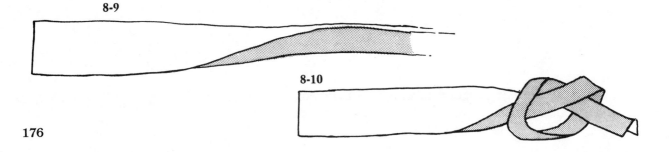

8-9

8-10

2. Sew the bottom seam wrong side out (figure 8-11). Turn (figures 8-12a and b). The distance between the knot and the tie point should be 2¼".

3. Squeeze a drop of glue into the inside of the knot. Trim the ribbon close to the knot.

4. Sew the tie to the shirt front (figure 8-8). The shirts and ties are so easy to make you can make several for the suit.

## ൠ Learn-to-Sew: Handkerchief Skirt or Strapless Dress and Cape (Color Plate 16)

MATERIALS

A handkerchief approximately 10" square
4" of elastic cord
12" piece of string or crochet cotton

STEP-BY-STEP: Strapless Dress or Skirt

1. Cut the handkerchief into two pieces (figure 8-13). The length of the skirt will vary according to the size of your handkerchief.

2. If your hankie has fancy edges, hand sew the center front (figure 8-14). If not, sew a regular seam.

3. Make a ⅜" casing at the top edge leaving an opening for the elastic (figure 8-14). Then insert the elastic cord with a small safety pin.

4. Tie the elastic cord to fit around the doll.

STEP-BY-STEP: Cape

1. Turn under a ⅜" casing at the top of the cape piece. Insert a piece of string or crochet thread with a small safety pin (figure 8-15).

2. Draw up the string around the doll's shoulders (figure 8-16).

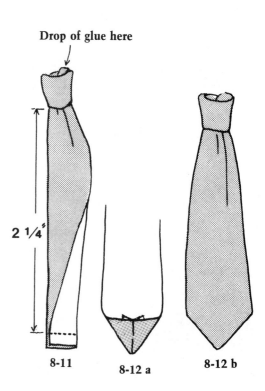

**Drop of glue here**

2 ¼'

8-11        8-12 a        8-12 b

Cape

Skirt or strapless dress

8-13

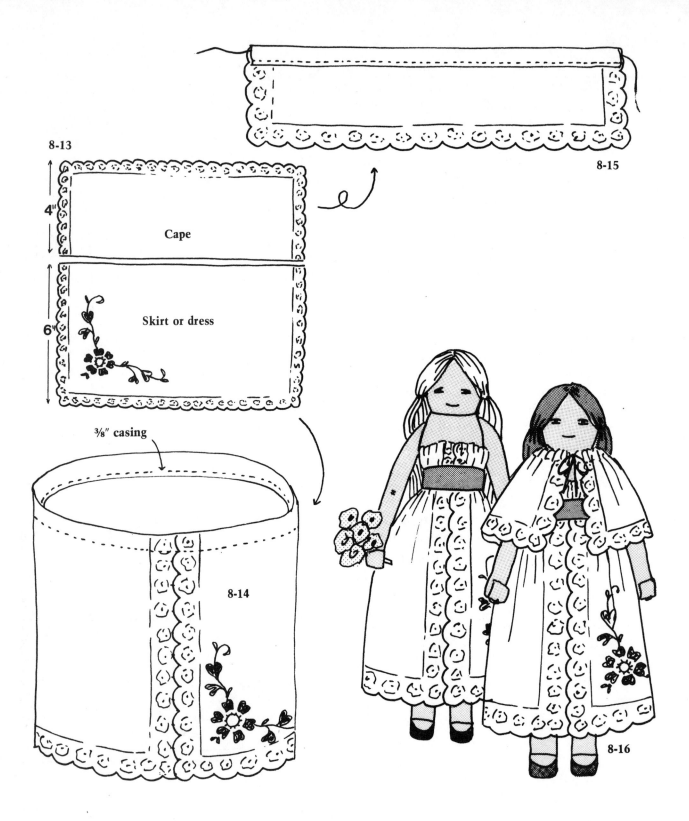

8-13

4"

Cape

6"

Skirt or dress

8-15

⅜" casing

8-14

8-16

## Wedding Suit (Color Plate 12)

**Jacket Pattern, page 180**

*Jacket with Tails*

### MATERIALS

Make the jacket out of black or grey felt.

### STEP-BY-STEP

1. With small machine stitches or by hand, sew close to the edge all around the jacket (figure 8-17).
2. With right sides together, sew the ¼″ side/sleeve seams. Clip (figure 8-18). Turn (figure 8-19).
3. Use a flower from the bride's bouquet for a boutonniere.

*Pants*

Make the wedding pants out of grey felt. Before you cut out the felt, draw stripes on it with a fine-tip black marker. Then follow the construction steps for the felt pants on page 149.

*Ascot*

### MATERIALS

9″ piece of ⅝″ wide white satin ribbon
Ball point pen or fine line marker

### STEP-BY-STEP

1. Make several fine line stripes 3″ long at the center of the ribbon, using a fine point marker or a ball point pen (figure 8-20).
2. Tie a loose overhand knot at the center (figure 8-21).
3. Place the ascot around the doll's neck (figure 8-22).

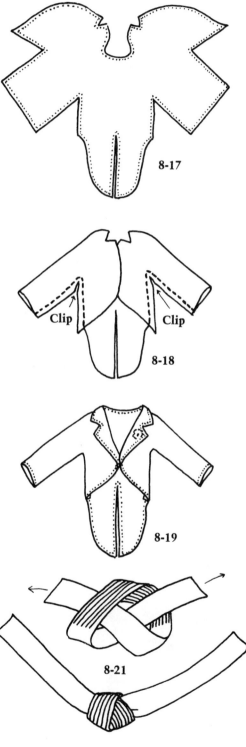

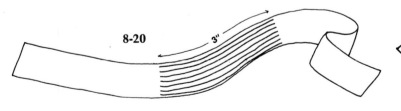

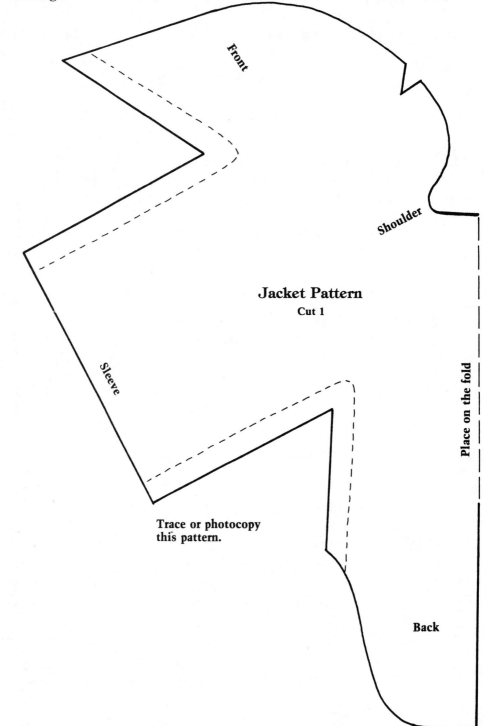

Front

Shoulder

**Jacket Pattern**
**Cut 1**

Sleeve

Place on the fold

**Trace or photocopy
this pattern.**

**Back**

MATERIALS

Small piece of grey felt
One snap
Gold cord or piece of a jewelry chain

STEP-BY-STEP

1. Sew on the snap at the X.
2. Sew on a length of gold cord or chain (figure 8-22).

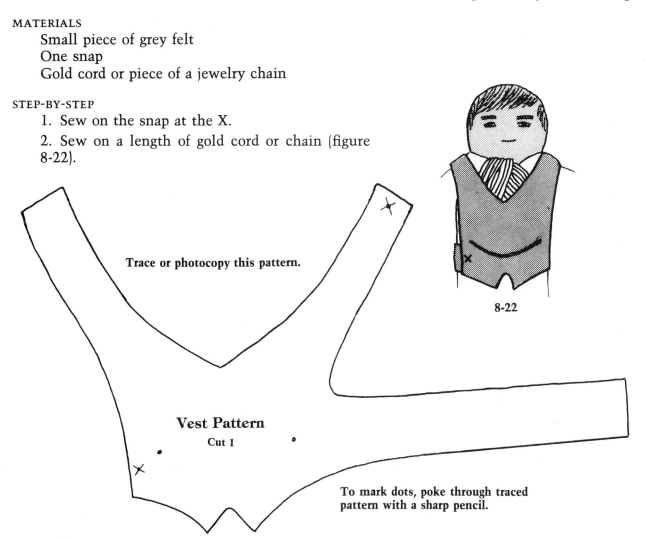

Trace or photocopy this pattern.

**Vest Pattern**
Cut 1

To mark dots, poke through traced pattern with a sharp pencil.

8-22

## Bride's Dress (Color Plate 12)

MATERIALS

8″ X 12″ piece of lightweight white fabric or a
    7½″ X 12″ section of a handkerchief
About 1¼ yards of 3″ wide lingerie-type lace
● Lace from an old slip might be just right. If you
    have narrow lace, just make more rows.
12″ piece of ⅝″ wide white satin ribbon
6″ of elastic cord
One snap
10″ square of white veiling or net

- Gentle washing will soften stiff net.

12″ of fine narrow lace

One white pipe cleaner

Bunch of artificial lilies of the valley (from a party favor or gift wrap store)

STEP-BY-STEP

1. If you are using fabric, hem the bottom raw edge.

2. Cut the lace into two 12″ lengths and one 18″ length.

3. Gather the 18″ length to 12″ and sew it to the fabric (figure 8-23).

4. Sew on a flat 12″ piece of lace, overlapping the first row by about a third (figure 8-23).

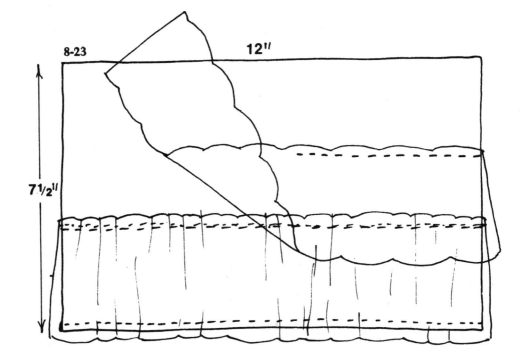

8-23    12″

7½″

- The 12″ piece of lace is sewn on flat but it will become ruffled when the top of the dress is gathered.

5. With right sides together, sew a ¼″ side seam.

6. Make a ⅜″ casing along the top edge, leaving an opening for the elastic (figure 8-24). Insert the elastic with a small safety pin.

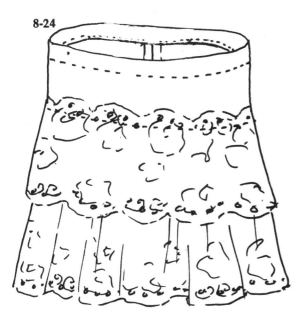

8-24

8-25

7. Tie the elastic to fit around the doll. Tie the satin ribbon around her waist (figure 8-25).

8. To make the shoulder ruffle, hem the side edges of the remaining 12″ piece of lace. Then stitch across the piece about 1″ from the top (figure 8-26) and gather (figure 8-27).

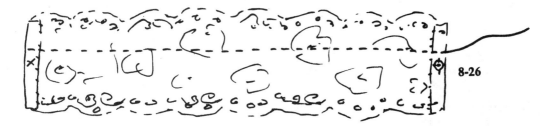

8-26

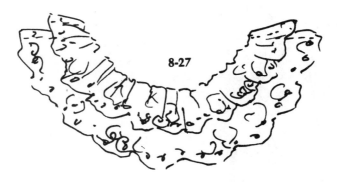

8-27

183

9. Fit the ruffle over the doll's shoulders and add a snap at the back (see figure 8-30).

10. To make the veil, cut out a 10″ diameter circle of netting. Sew the fine lace around the edge of the circle (figure 8-28). Bend the pipe cleaner into a circle to fit your doll's head. Sew a sprig of lily of the valley to the pipe cleaner circle, then sew the circle onto the veil (figure 8-28).

11. Bend the lily of the valley into a cascading bouquet (figure 8-29).

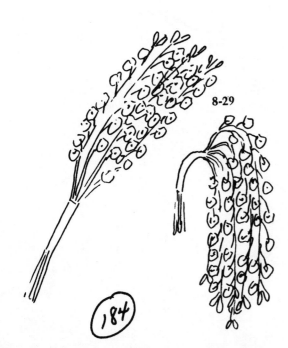

8-28

8-29

8-30

184

## Fancy Shirt (Color Plates 10 and 17)

**Fancy Shirt Pattern, page 186**

This fancy shirt might be worn by a prince, a rock star, or a space traveller! Girl dolls can wear the shirt either with the collar or with a scoop neckline.

MATERIALS
  Fabric
  Two snaps

STEP-BY-STEP

1. Cut out the fabric using the white glue technique, page 145.

2. With the fabric right sides together, sew ¼" side and sleeve seams. Clip (figure 8-31). Turn.

3. Fold down the collar (figure 8-32).

4. Gather the sleeves at the bottom with a long running stitch or turn up the cuffs (figure 8-32).

5. Sew on the snaps.

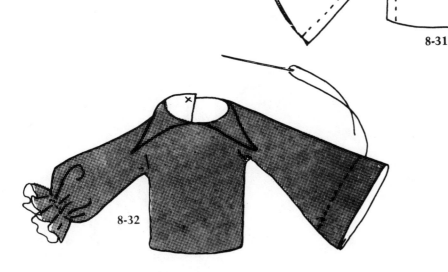

8-31

8-32

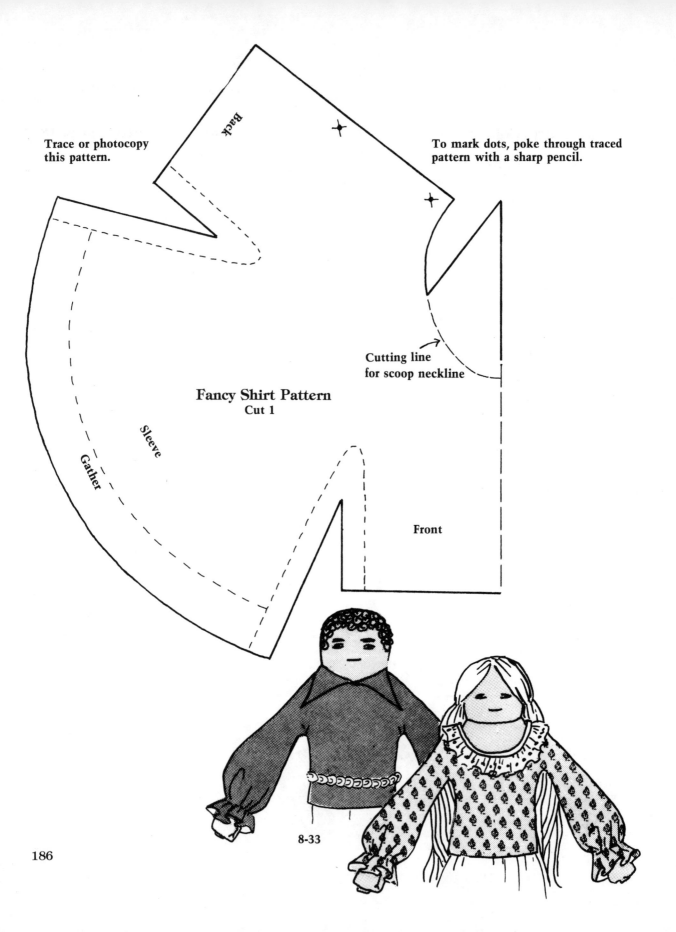

Trace or photocopy
this pattern.

To mark dots, poke through traced
pattern with a sharp pencil.

Back

**Fancy Shirt Pattern**
Cut 1

Sleeve

Gather

Cutting line
for scoop neckline

Front

8-33

186

## ❧ Learn-to-Sew: Prince's Tabard (Color Plate 18)

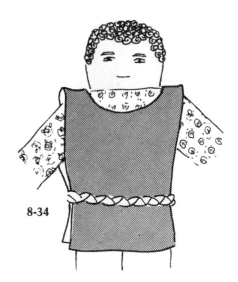

MATERIALS

Small piece of felt
6″ of metallic braid
One snap for the belt

STEP-BY-STEP

1. Cut out the felt using the pattern and put the tabard on the doll. There's no sewing to do!

2. Add a belt of metallic braid with a snap for fastening it on (figure 8-34). Or you can make a medieval-looking chain belt with a section of links from an old bracelet or necklace.

8-34

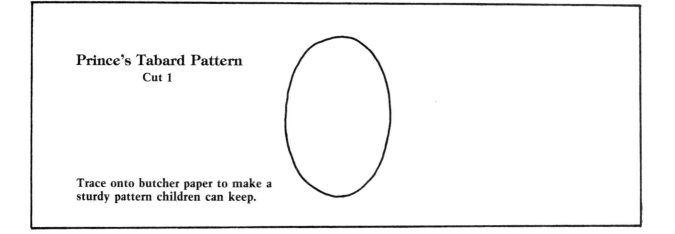

**Prince's Tabard Pattern**
Cut 1

**Trace onto butcher paper to make a sturdy pattern children can keep.**

## Fairy Tale Gown (Color Plate 16)

MATERIALS

A square handkerchief, about 12″ X 12″
6″ of elastic thread
10″ piece of 1″–1½″ wide lace (optional, for neck ruffle)
12″ piece of ribbon (optional, for sash)
One snap (optional)

STEP-BY-STEP

1. Cut out the gown sections according to figure 8-35.

● The measurements shown are for a 12″ square handkerchief. Alter the measurements to suit the size of your hankie.

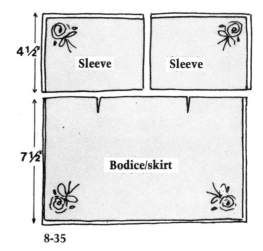

4½″
Sleeve    Sleeve

7½″
Bodice/skirt

8-35

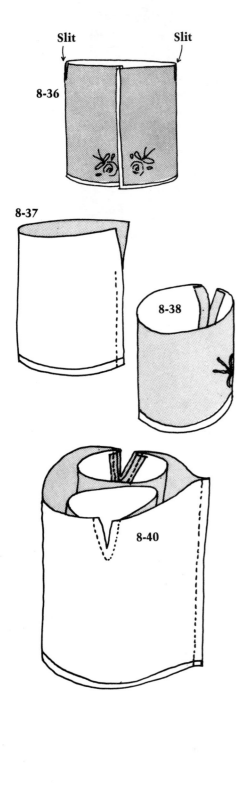

**8-36**

Slit    Slit

**8-37**

**8-38**

**8-40**

2. Fold the bodice/skirt section and make 1¼" slits at the sides (figure 8-36).

3. With right sides together, sew the sleeve seam leaving the top 1½" open (figure 8-37). Turn (figure 8-38).

4. Sew the sleeve to the bodice/skirt (figure 8-39).

**8-39**

5. Sew the center front seam right sides together (figure 8-40).

• If the hankie has a fancy edge, overlap the front edges and hand stitch them closed (see figure 8-43).

6. Sew a ⅜" casing along the top edge (figure 8-41) leaving an opening for the elastic. Insert the elastic with a small safety pin.

Opening for elastic

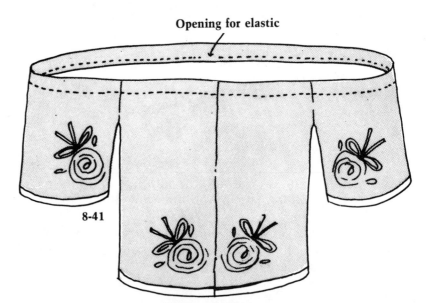

**8-41**

7. The dress can be finished in several different ways.

- Place the ruffled lace around the doll's neck over the dress. Hem the raw edges of the lace and add a snap (figure 8-42).
- Gather the sleeves at the wrist with small running stitches.

8-42

8-43

# 9
# Lovable Animals

When children come to visit in my home their eyes usually light up at the sight of all the dollhouses sitting invitingly around the room. They run to play with this one or that, choosing perhaps by their favorite colors or by which accessories they spot first. Most of them, however, come to a decided halt in front of the bear house. The soft little bears—Mama and Papa and their twin children—have a way of capturing the hearts of nearly everyone, young and old.

I hope you'll decide to make these little creatures. They're very easy to sew and are good fun to play with. I think you'll become awfully fond of them and enjoy showing them off to your visitors.

The pets included in this chapter have also been known to steal hearts away. Looking so cute and realistic, they're fun little fellows to have around, too.

## BEAR FAMILY (Color Plate 20)

MATERIALS

Three 9" X 12" pieces of felt, brown or tan
A scrap of white felt for nose patches
Black seed beads for eyes and nose (three for each bear), or black embroidery floss
Brown or tan thread to match the felt
White and black thread for the face
Polyester fiberfill for stuffing
One ¼" snap for each bear

STEP-BY-STEP

1. Pencil around the patterns (see the layouts, figure 9-1). Cut out the front head, torso, legs, and arms on the cutting line. Do not cut out the back yet.

2. Poke a pencil through the pattern to transfer face and shoulder markings (figure 9-2).

3. Trace and cut out the white nose patch. Hand stitch it onto the face about ⅔ of the way around with white thread. Stuff it with a tiny bit of fiberfill. Sew the rest of the way around the nose. Sew the mouth and nose line with black thread. Then sew on a seed bead nose and eyes with the same black thread (figure 9-3). You can make French knot eyes and nose with floss if you prefer.

Mama and Papa bear

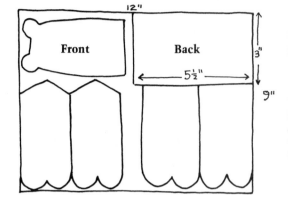

Two Baby bears

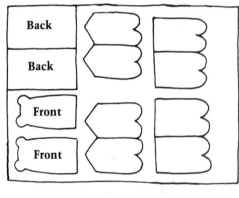

9-1

**Bear Family Patterns, pages 194 and 195**

9-2      9-3

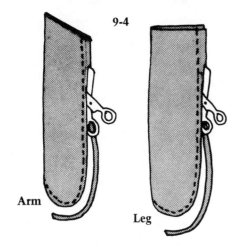

9-4

Arm

Leg

4. Sew all bear sections right side out. Fold each arm and leg, pin, and topstitch around each one ¼" from the edge. Trim to ⅛" (figure 9-4).

5. Sew on the hand snaps. Fold and sew the hands (figure 9-5).

6. Sew the legs to the front piece only (figure 9-6). Backstitch at each end for strength.

7. Insert the arms between the front piece and the uncut back fabric (figure 9-7). Pin all layers and sew around the edges ⅛" from the front piece edge. Sew both across and around the ears (figure 9-7).

8. Trim off the excess back fabric to match the front edge. Be careful not to cut off the arms (figure 9-7).

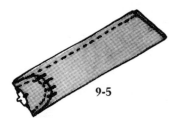

9-5

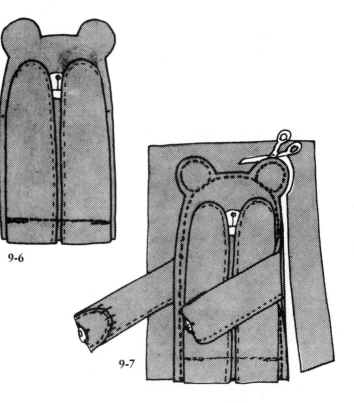

9-6

9-7

9. Stuff the body. Then tuck in the bottom and hand sew it closed (figure 9-8).

Brushing lightly with a fingernail brush gives the bears a natural furry look. Don't overdo this because it can wear away the felt. Practice first on a scrap.

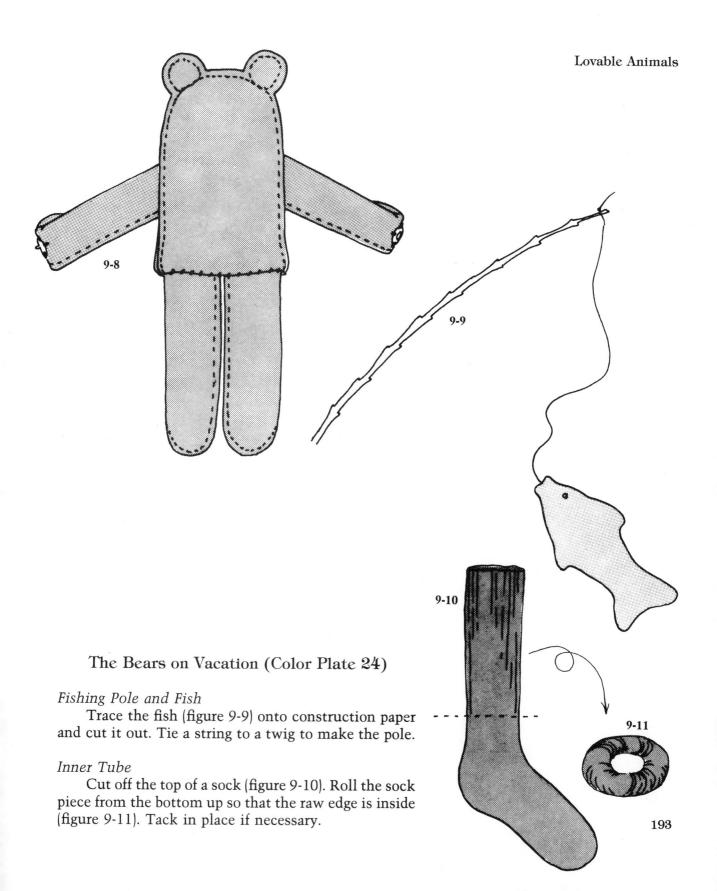

**9-8**

**9-9**

**9-10**

**9-11**

## The Bears on Vacation (Color Plate 24)

*Fishing Pole and Fish*

Trace the fish (figure 9-9) onto construction paper and cut it out. Tie a string to a twig to make the pole.

*Inner Tube*

Cut off the top of a sock (figure 9-10). Roll the sock piece from the bottom up so that the raw edge is inside (figure 9-11). Tack in place if necessary.

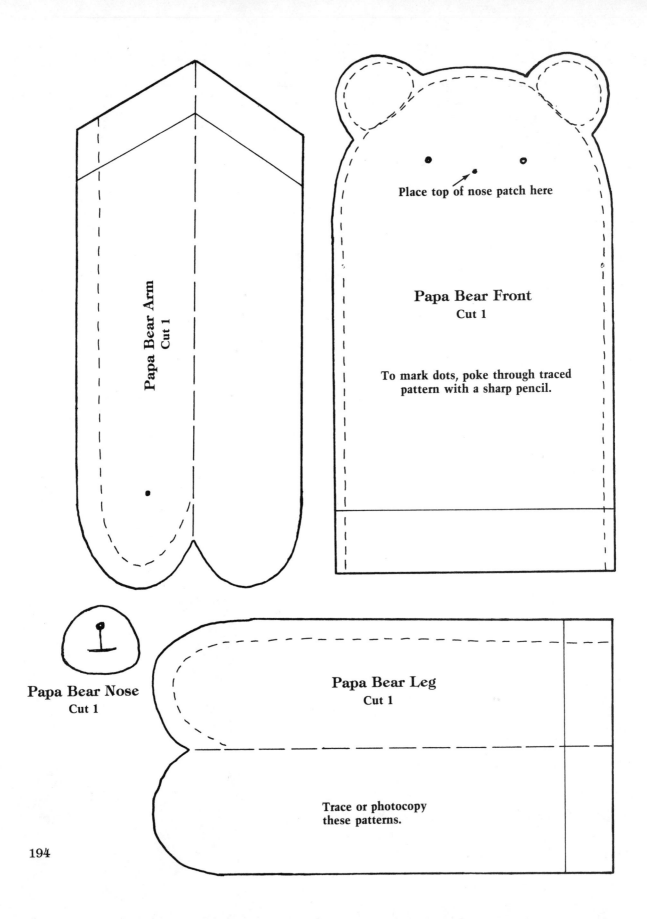

Papa Bear Arm
Cut 1

Papa Bear Front
Cut 1

Place top of nose patch here

To mark dots, poke through traced
pattern with a sharp pencil.

Papa Bear Nose
Cut 1

Papa Bear Leg
Cut 1

Trace or photocopy
these patterns.

194

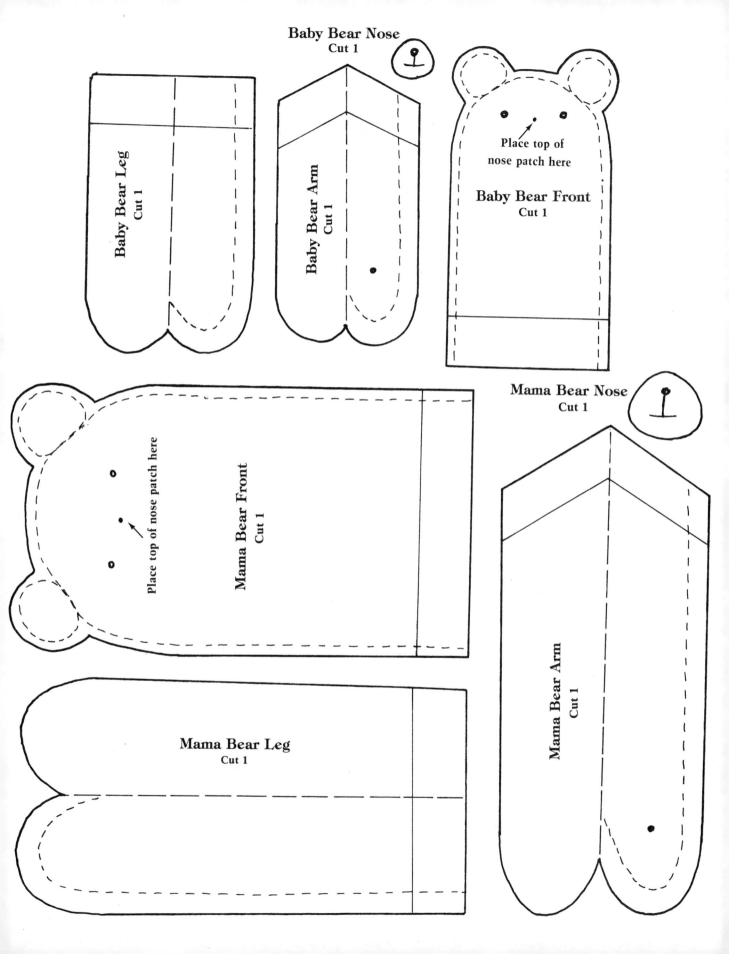

**Baby Bear Nose**
Cut 1

**Baby Bear Leg** Cut 1

**Baby Bear Arm** Cut 1

**Baby Bear Front**
Cut 1

Place top of
nose patch here

**Mama Bear Nose**
Cut 1

**Mama Bear Front**
Cut 1

Place top of nose patch here

**Mama Bear Arm**
Cut 1

**Mama Bear Leg**
Cut 1

# PETS

If your doll family is not complete without pets, you'll be happy to know you can make cats and dogs galore out of little pieces of fake fur. These lovable pets are simple to make.

### MATERIALS

You can find 6" X 12" strips of fake fur in hobby shops and five-and-tens. Use black seed beads for the eyes. You'll need a pipe cleaner for the cat.

## Dog (Color Plate 17)

### STEP-BY-STEP

1. Cut a 5½" X 4" piece of fake fur with the nap direction as illustrated (figure 9-12).

2. Fold up a 1½" hem at the back (figure 9-13). (This large hem actually stuffs the dog.)

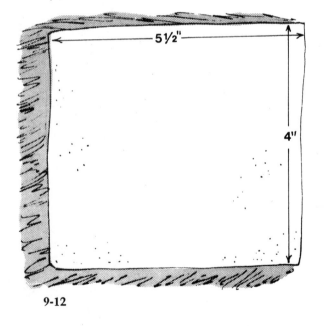

9-12

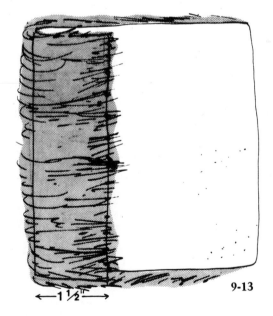

9-13

←—1½"—→

3. Fold lengthwise, right sides together, and hand sew with a backstitch to within ½" of the fold and edge (figure 9-14).

4. Turn right side out and sew the bottom and legs (figure 9-15).

5. With a comb, separate out a few fur strands to make ears (figure 9-16). Rub a little white glue on them. Bend the fur back for round ears or trim it for pointed ears.

6. Sew on seed beads for eyes (figure 9-16).

7. Comb the dog. Trim under the chin if necessary.

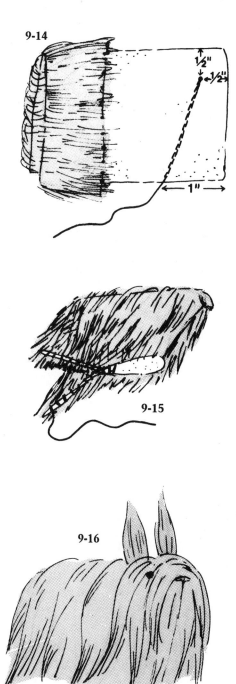

**9-14**

½"

½"

1"

**9-15**

**9-16**

# Cat (Color Plate 17)

The cat is made the same as the dog, but the fur piece you start out with is smaller. Follow Steps 1, 2, and 3 for making the dog.

4. Cut the tail piece 5″ X ½″ again following the nap direction indicated (figure 9-19). Sew a pipe cleaner inside the tail strip for a bendable tail (figure 9-20).

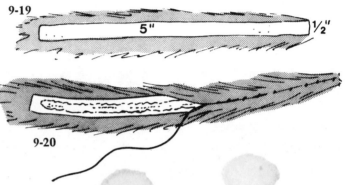

**9-19**

**9-20**

5. Sew the tail to the body leaving 3½″ on the outside (figure 9-21).

Follow Steps 4 through 7 for the dog.

8. To make whiskers, thread a bristle from a brush or a broom onto a needle and insert it so that each bristle sticks out on both sides of the cat's face (figure 9-23). Put a little glue at the base of the whiskers to hold them in place.

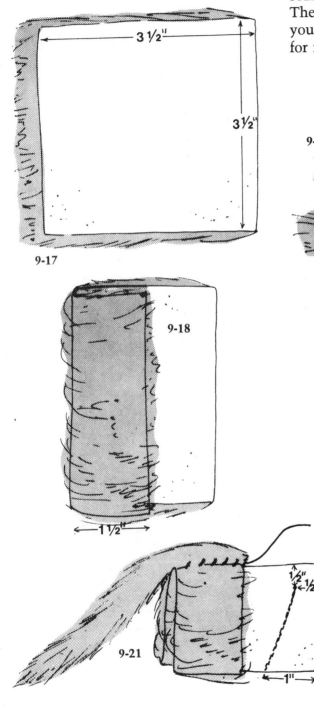

**9-17**

**9-18**

**9-21**

**9-22**

**9-23**

# Index